GO NEXT-LEVEL

GO NEXT-LEVEL

9 QUESTIONS YOU NEED TO ANSWER TO GET **ABSOLUTE CLARITY** ON WHAT MATTERS MOST, AND FULFILL EVERYTHING YOU WANT IN **BUSINESS** AND **LIFE**

QUENTIN HAFNER

CONTENTS

1		**INTRODUCTION**
16	*1*	**WHAT DO YOU WANT?** ARCHITECTING YOUR IDEAL LIFE
36	*2*	**WHY DO YOU WANT IT?** KNOWING WHAT BREAKS YOUR HEART AND WHAT PISSES YOU OFF
56	*3*	**WHAT DO YOU NEED TO SAY "YES" TO?** BECOMING A NEXT-LEVEL RISK-TAKER
80	*4*	**WHAT DO YOU NEED TO SAY "NO" TO?** RUTHLESSLY PROTECT YOUR MOST PRECIOUS ASSET
102	*5*	**HOW ARE YOU GOING TO SAVE THE WORLD?** IDENTIFYING YOUR UNIQUE MILLION-DOLLAR MISSION

128 **6 WHO IS GOING WITH YOU?**
BUILDING YOUR UNSTOPPABLE LIFE-TEAM

154 **7 WHO DO YOU THINK YOU ARE?**
DEVELOPING AN UNSHAKABLE MINDSET

178 **8 WHAT IS THE PLAN?**
GETTING FOCUSED WITH GO NEXT-LEVEL GOALS

204 **9 HOW ARE YOU GOING TO GET THERE?**
DEVELOPING THE GO-NEXT-LEVEL HABITS

229 **CONCLUSION**
START GOING NEXT-LEVEL, TODAY

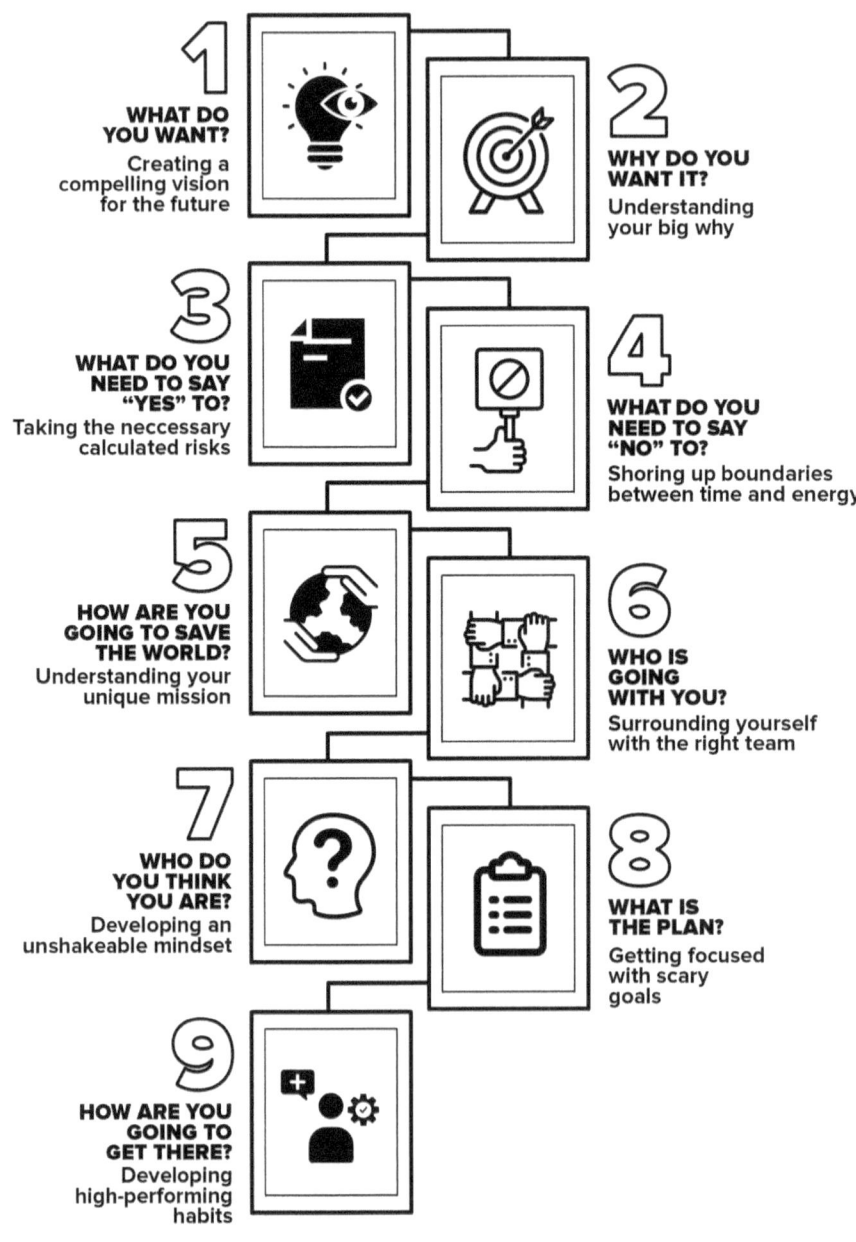

INTRODUCTION

THE BLUEPRINT GUIDING YOU TO THE NEXT LEVEL

If you're anything like me, no one ever taught you exactly what it takes to actually live an ultra-successful life and *fulfill* everything you want. You didn't learn how to do this in school from teachers, and even though your parents wanted the best for you, there's a good chance you weren't given any formal instruction on how to accomplish such a lofty goal. What does it actually take to truly live a life of huge success and deeply meaningful significance? What is the roadmap you need to follow if you want to truly optimize your business and your life, and leave the biggest and most memorable impact possible?

Make it to the end of this book and you'll find the answers. Do the work I suggest, and an ultra-successful life awaits just around the corner.

If you're reading this book, then you're the type of person who's already made it pretty far on the path to success. By most standards, you're doing good. Even without formal instruction on how to achieve **massive success**, you've set out to pursue it. You believed in yourself enough to charge forward; committed to making the most of life. At some point, you felt that rush deep in your bones that said, *'I'm going to make something of myself, if it's the last thing I do.'* You saw clearly that no one else was going to do it for you ... and with a beautiful chip on your shoulder, you went after it.

Fueled by grit, ambition, hard work, and resilience, you've made incredible progress. But here's the problem: Grit, ambition, hard work, and resilience are necessary qualities to achieve success, but they only take you so far. There's something missing. You don't know exactly what it is, but you know there's another level of success attainable to you. It won't happen the same way as the first time. It won't come from outworking everyone, staying late, and putting in the extra hours. Achieving the next level requires a new game plan and a fresh map. That map is now in your hands.

And, there's another type of person reading this book. Maybe you're someone climbing your way to the top, and you want to know how to get there in the most expeditious way possible and avoid all the painful pitfalls. I get it—not everyone feels like they've 'made it' just yet. You might be feeling stuck, working what feels like a meaningless job. You might feel like you're doing things that 'just don't matter' and you haven't figured out how to find your breakthrough. Don't walk away just yet! Please don't think, 'This book is for other people, but not me.' This book is exactly for you too. All are welcome on this journey, if you're willing to do the work.

This book is a roadmap to the summit, to dizzying heights of success, where only a few will arrive and where most people are even afraid to dream about. The few that dare to dream and make it aren't any better than you and I, they simply followed the map with dedication, precision, and **tackled the fears** that keep people from realizing their full potential. Implement the strategies contained within this book, and everything you see yourself becoming will come to fruition. The tools and exercises inside this book are designed to maximize what you're capable of. You will unlock your legacy, find clarity around your deepest purpose in life, and go to the next level.

 To be crystal clear, this is not a book about happiness.

This is a book about you, reaching your God-given potential, of which, happiness becomes a by-product. This book is about saying "no" to playing small because the world needs you to start showing up playing big.

If you want to accelerate your growth, then this book is for you.

If you feel stuck, and you're just not sure of what direction you need to go next, this book is for you. This book is for anyone who intuitively knows there is another gear and another level where untapped potential can be obtained. This is *the guide* on how to get there.

A 9-STEP BLUEPRINT TO GO NEXT-LEVEL

In this book, I'm going to show you a nine-step Blueprint to crush life on all fronts; professionally and personally. If you follow this Blueprint, you cannot fail- *this is my promise*. Let me say that again: If you follow this nine-step Blueprint, you will reach new levels of fulfillment previously unattainable to you. You have the possibility to reach all of your dreams, all your goals, and get everything you want in life. You cannot fail. That is my money-back guarantee for reading this book.

But let me be clear, it's not going to be easy. This might be the hardest book you've ever read. It won't be academically difficult, but it will still make your head spin and will stop you in your tracks by making you think. And think deeply. I'm going to ask you to dig deep and discover things about yourself that you didn't know were there. I'm going to ask you to look at yourself, your life, and your career through *superhuman eyes*. I'll ask you to go beyond any limit you've ever had placed on yourself.

But the rewards are worth the struggle: clarity, purpose, financial gain, love, freedom, and a mission-driven life.

SUCCESS LEAVES CLUES

As I write this book, I have been privileged to coach and consult some of the most successful people on the planet. With over 20,000 hours and nearly two decades coaching high-achievers to move past stuck plateaus and helping them go to the next level in business and life, I have worked with the world's elite; from World-Series winning pitchers, to CEOs of Fortune 500 companies.

I've also seen the darker side of success. The people that "have it all", and have nothing at the same time. They may have private planes, boats, and 2nd houses scattered around the world, but they are desperately miserable, and on the edge of quitting in life.

What is the difference between these two groups of people?

You'll learn important lessons from people who have achieved so much materially, only to find they over-rotated in their occupational pursuits and paid a heavy, regretful price in the end. I'll show you how to find that sweet spot between life and business where you can maximize your ability to fulfill everything you want, and at the same time never lose sight of your deeper calling in life that gives you a rich sense of satisfaction.

 Because one without the other is no life at all.

For the last 20 years I've been obsessed with answering the question: "How do we help people move from "*good*" to "*unstoppable*"? It seemed relatively easy to help people move out of a challenging spot of their life and business into a relatively good spot, but it was much less clear how to help people get to an elite place in their life and business. I became obsessed with answering this question. As someone who always sees potential in everyone I meet, I wanted to see people who were content making the varsity team in highschool get *so good* that the major leagues came calling. And I want the same thing for you.

So I pushed all my chips to the center of the table and made this goal the focus of my work and developed Skyward Success Coaching™, my flagship coaching methodology, which blended three elements: 1. Principles of high-performance and high-achievement, 2. Results-based transformational coaching, and 3. My education, experience, and background with psychology.

I had one chief aim; ***help people go to entirely new levels in life and***

business. I achieved it for myself in my own world, so I knew I could teach it to anyone else who was willing to learn. I have been obsessed with helping people reach their greatest potential, and I refused to settle for allowing anyone in my sphere to live **"good-enough lives"**.

THE WORLD NEEDS YOU TO GO NEXT-LEVEL

Imagine a world where you were living to your greatest potential, doing exactly what your natural talents and giftings had afforded you, and bearing the fruit of doing exactly what you were meant to do. Reaching **all your goals** and living a passion-filled life with deep meaning and purpose. Can you imagine that? If I was to meet you in person, **this is** the potential I would see in you. I would see your great capabilities that would point you in the direction of living the life you were supposed to live, and I would be obsessed with helping you actualize it. If I met you in person, *I would see* your great potential.

But the more important question is, *would you see* your own great potential? Would I hear it in your voice, or perceive it from your confidence? Would I be able to perceive your strength and power? Would I notice how clear you are about yourself and where you are going in life?

Or would I see someone who was uncertain, lacking clarity, or living a life of subtle resignation that was masked by fake smiles, materialism, and shallow relationships?

You have to start by acknowledging the truth—we haven't been given a clear and actionable Blueprint to get what we want. We've been told, 'Work hard, save money, go to college, get a good job.' And typically that's about it. And of course, that's not bad advice, but it doesn't lead anyone to optimization and maximum fulfillment. Even if we make a pile of money following that simple formula, the material gain never fully satisfies. Without a better actionable Blueprint, it's like trying to find your way around New York City with a map of

Los Angeles. The first step on the road to higher levels of success is to start by admitting that we need a *new map.*

The traditional advice we receive gets us only so far, and eventually we hit something I call the **Early Peak Plateau**. It's the place we land after we apply everything we know about hard work, dedication, being resilient, and grit. It's the old map that gets us to a certain point. But the map is incomplete. It doesn't show us anything about fulfillment, legacy, being mission-driven, and making a real difference in the world. When we hit the plateau, we feel fatigued, tired, burned out, and ready to throw in the towel, but we can't because at this point we have obligations. So, we do what most people do, we put our heads down and we grind harder, using the same methods and techniques that landed us on the plateau in the first place. And this is where most people reside; painfully stuck on this plateau.

The Go Next-Level Blueprint is the solution to get us off the plateau and move to the next level in all areas of our life. The next level is where life, business, making money, and relationships get more fun, enlivening and prosperous.

THE EARLY PEAK PLATEAU

We don't have to look far to see people stuck on the plateau. They're struggling to find meaning, they're doing tasks that don't suit them, and sometimes they are just making ends meet. They don't have a clear path for reaching their full potential. When people are stuck on the plateau, this shows up as depression, burnout, fatigue, and a vast onset of other psychological problems. People want to find greater levels of success, but they don't know how to get off the plateau. Escape feels elusive and out of reach. People say, "it must be for them over there … but not for me". Of course, that isn't true. Success and fulfillment is available for absolutely anyone willing to do the internal work and right kind of heavy lifting to get there.

This book is born out of my privilege of learning from where

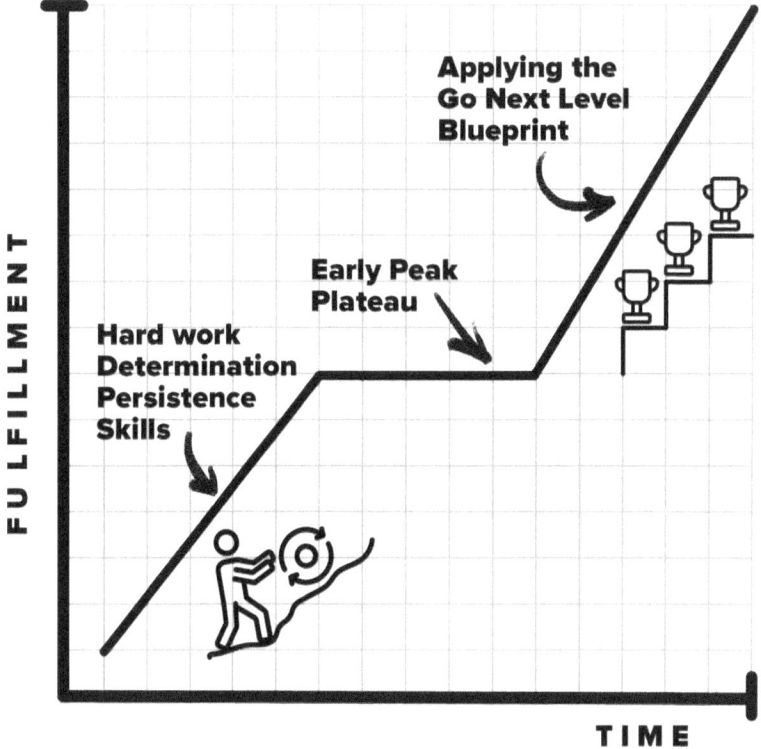

successful people have gone right, and where they've gone wrong. I've had the privilege to coach individuals and business teams when they have reached mountain tops of extreme success seemingly overnight, and conversely, I've witnessed those who've gotten stuck on a plateau and unwilling to launch to a higher level. This book is a culmination of learning from both sides of life experiences.

GET READY TO LAUNCH

When you follow the Go Next-Level Blueprint, you can catapult your life to unimaginable heights. You'll notice renewed excitement and enthusiasm about your life, and you'll start accomplishing all of your goals with unprecedented bursts of energy and drive. Getting back in the driver's seat of your life, taking control, and being honest about your dreams is the starting place for the Blueprint. This book is about taking back control of your life, reclaiming your personal autonomy, and unlocking your personal empowerment so you can get what you want and **become** who you were made to be.

When we're not actually in control of living our own lives and doing what is most meaningful and essential, we will always struggle. Mental Illness is increasing everywhere around us. People are suffering from depression, anxiety, and addiction at unprecedented rates. People everywhere are doing work they don't love, burned out, have lost meaning and purpose in their day-to-day lives, and feel less-than-hopeful about having something better.

But even though people are struggling, the silver lining is that the cracks in the vase of the common and typical way of going through life and business have been illuminated. Many people are realizing that the life they thought they had to live is up for question, in exchange for something more impactful. They are allowed to pursue deeper meaning and purpose in their life. This book will teach you to figure out your purpose, your path, and your goals—and then with patience, belief in yourself, and dedication to your plan, you'll fulfill all you want and more. This book is medicine needed to kill any speckle of apathy about life.

When we follow the Blueprint inside this book, we gain essential clarity about ourselves, what matters most to us, what brings us the most internal and external sense of freedom, and the practical steps needed to reach our greatest potential.

SUCCESS IS JUST DECISION MAKING

No matter where you find yourself in your current circumstances, you will find personal application inside this book. It doesn't matter if you're a hungry entrepreneur looking to take your business to a new level, a retiring CEO looking for a change, or a stay-at-home mother wanting to reinvent herself after the kids are grown. This book is a Blueprint that we *all have to follow* if we want to live great lives and achieve what is optimal for us.

Life, at its core, is a series of decisions. Every time you say 'Yes' to one thing, you say 'No' to something else. Every day, we make thousands of decisions. Should we do this thing, or do that thing? Success in getting unstuck from the Early Peak Plateau and launching to the next level is the ability to make *the right decisions* that separate the successful from the less successful. That's it.

Most decisions are rarely between 'good and bad.' They're actually between 'good and less good'. We tend to think of decision making in a black and white way as if people make decisions between good things and bad things, but this is actually quite rare. Most people are making decisions between *two good* options.

But, with two good options, one decision is going to get you off the plateau, and the other is going to keep you on it. We need a decision making tool to help us see clearly how we can make the **best** decision, and not just any good decision. To Go Next-Level, we simply have to make more of these best and great decisions, and that's what we'll learn how to do in this book.

Today, you will make thousands of decisions. Will those decisions exponentially increase your probability of greater levels of success? Or will those decisions keep you on the plateau? Once you understand the contents of the Blueprint in this book, your decision making process and capabilities will be forever changed.

A CLEAR ROADMAP FOR SUCCESS

The 9-step process in this book will guide you through nine questions that, if answered, will give you unbridled motivation, clarity, and an uncanny jolt you need to accomplish very ambitious goals.

In **Chapter One,** you'll answer, *What do you want?* We'll dissect this simple but complicated question and you'll learn how to architect your Ideal Life. In **Chapter Two,** we'll look at *Why do you want it?* You'll learn the vital importance of having a Big Why and getting clear on your purpose. In **Chapter Three,** you'll get clear on, *What do you need to say "yes" to?* We'll look at how to decrease your risk-averseness by increasing your ability to seek and say yes to new opportunities.

In **Chapter Four** we'll pivot to, *What do you need to say "no" to?* You'll learn how to cut every distraction from your life that keeps you from going to the next level. **In Chapter Five**, you'll get the biggest question yet, *How are you going to save the world?* You'll discover how to start getting aligned with your unique Mission in the world. **Chapter Six** is the perfect follow up by asking, *Who is going with you?* You'll name your Life-Team and learn how to rally the right people around you in your bid to Go Next-Level.

Chapter Seven will challenge you to consider, *Who do you think you are?* You'll learn key mindset principles needed to master to Go Next-Level. As the 9-step Blueprint narrows, **Chapter Eight** will ask you, *What is the plan?* In it, I'll share the best goal-setting tips I know to help you create a foolproof plan. And lastly, **Chapter Nine** asks you to consider, *How are you going to get there?* This is where we take everything we've learned in the preceding eight chapters, and have it culminated with high-performance habits so you can Go Next-Level.

In addition to the information inside each chapter, I've also included practical exercises along the way you can work through on your journey of going to the next level. I always encourage readers to read the book once through, then come back through a second time to put everything into action.

Please visit: **www.QuentinHafner.com/GoNextLevel** to find additional digital resources to help you reach the Go Next-Level summit.

WHAT IS YOUR DEFINITION OF SUCCESS?

For all of us, we each have a different definition of success and going to the next level. For some, it's achieving a certain net worth. For others, it's reinventing themselves in the second half of life. And for some, it's reaching that seemingly elusive place of contentment that has been missing throughout life. The promise of this book is that it will help you define success as it matters most to you, and show you a map for how to achieve it. On a practical note, I will use the word 'success' throughout the book to refer to *your definition* of success, because that is the only definition of success that matters.

 The only important version of "success" is the one that matters to you.

Success is personal, unique, and I want to help you reach the summit of your own definition.

A fair warning; This book is not going to be easy. It's not difficult from an academic standpoint; this book is fairly straightforward and conversational. It's challenging because it prompts you to truly take the time to look at yourself honestly and thoroughly. This book is not a get-rich-quick scheme. This book is not a get-happy-now scheme. This book is going to ask you to look at every element of your life in a thought-provoking way. Taking short cuts isn't an option. However, if you're up for the challenge, this book will change your life forever in the most transformative ways—*no matter your circumstances.*

THE DEVIL WANTS YOU TO WAIT

If I were going to describe the devil, that spiritual force that causes pain, havoc, and regret, I would describe him as a master of convincing people to wait on their dreams. More pain and turmoil is caused in life from people living lives of quiet desperation, or sometimes not-so-quiet desperation. But inside every person who suffers stuck on a plateau feeling hopeless about creating a better future, is an Ideal Life that is awaiting them.

All of life's problems are the same at their core; a lack of clarity about what matters most, and lacking a plan to get to where you want to go. And this is where the devil comes in. Because I believe the greatest tragedy in life is to put things off that will help us fulfill our potential. We say, "I'll do it tomorrow". Or, "I'll get to it next month". Or "I'll start making those changes when......". If the devil exists, surely he exists to keep people stuck and waiting on making critical changes.

This book is for the people sick of waiting. Action-takers, world-changers and overcomers. If you want to squeeze every last drop of what life has to offer, you have no business sitting on your hands. And if you want to know a key source of any person's unhappiness ... it is *failing* to take action.

And so ... you will also be tempted to delay taking action in reading this book and applying its contents. You will tell yourself you're too busy, and that you don't have the time, or that other things are more important. Please, don't do that. There isn't anything more important in this world than you discovering what matters most to you and offering the world the best version of yourself. It will make you a better business owner, a better friend, a better spouse, a better parent, a better leader. Pursuing a life that is most meaningful and rewarding to you is the *opposite of selfish*. It's selfish not to, because other people around you suffer when you're not living the life you're meant to live.

 Don't let the devil whisper in your ear telling you tomorrow is a better day. Today is the only day any of us are guaranteed.

THE BEGINNING OF THE REST OF YOUR LIFE

Okay, my friend, today is Day One. Today is when we begin the process of Going Next-Level. No longer will we be content living on any Early Peak Plateaus, accepting the status quo. Today is the day we begin taking the reins of our lives and actually architect the life we want.

Follow along as we embark on a journey of helping you get off any and all plateaus, to a place of great clarity where you feel enthusiastic about new possibilities. Grab a pen, grab your journal, and get ready to go from zero to 100. Let's Go Next-Level!

INTRODUCTION KEY-TAKEAWAYS

→ This book is for two types of readers. Reader one is the person who's already made it pretty far on the path to success. By most standards, you're doing good. Even without formal instruction on how to achieve massive success, you've set out to pursue it. You believed in yourself enough to charge forward; committed to making the most of life. But there's something missing. You don't know exactly what it is, but you know there's another level of success attainable to you.

→ Or you're reader two. Maybe you're someone climbing your way to the top, and you want to know how to get there in the most expeditious way possible and avoid all the painful pitfalls. You might be feeling stuck, working what feels like a meaningless job. You might feel like you're doing things that 'just don't matter' and you haven't figured out how to find your breakthrough. **This book is exactly for you too**.

→ **This is not a book about happiness**. This is a book about you, reaching your God-given potential, of which, happiness becomes a by-product. This book is about saying "no" to playing small because the world needs you to start showing up playing big.

→ We haven't been given a clear and actionable blueprint to get what we want. We've been told, 'Work hard, save money, go to college, get a good job.' And typically, that's about it. And of course, that's not bad advice, but it doesn't lead anyone to optimization and maximum fulfillment.

→ Even if we make a pile of money following that simple formula, the material gain never fully satisfies. This book is about optimizing every part of our lives that matters to us.

→ The traditional advice we receive gets us only so far, and eventually we hit something I call the **Early Peak Plateau**. The Go Next-Level Blueprint is the solution to get us off the plateau and move to the next level in all areas of our life. The next level is where life, business, making money, and relationships get more fun, enlivening and prosperous.

→ The promise of this book is that it will help you define success as it matters most to you, and show you a map for how to achieve it. I will use the word 'success' throughout the book to refer to your definition of success, because that is the only definition of success that matters. The only important version of "success" is **the one that matters to you**.

CHAPTER ONE

WHAT DO YOU WANT?

GO NEXT-LEVEL BLUEPRINT STEP #1:

ARCHITECTING YOUR IDEAL LIFE

> If you don't design your own life plan, chances are you'll fall into someone else's plan.
>
> **JIM ROHN**

THE GO NEXT-LEVEL BLUEPRINT

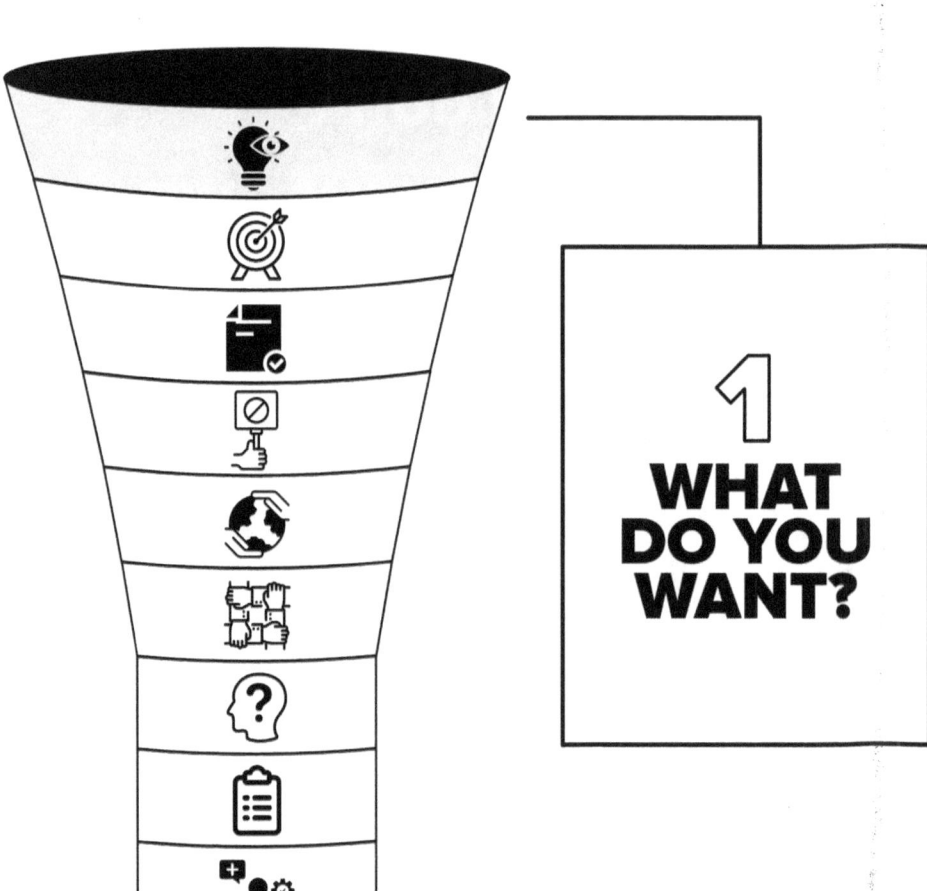

1

WHAT DO YOU WANT?

WE HAVE TO KNOW WHERE WE ARE GOING

Imagine a 4-day backpacking trip through the Eastern Sierra mountains where you finish the hike at a majestic, 100-foot glacial waterfall. Think of this backpacking trip as a metaphor for your life. Before you go, you'd make lots of plans. You'd look at a lot of maps. You'd ask for advice from people who have done the trip. You'd make sure you have enough food and water. And likely, you'd ask the right people to go with you to make the trip more enjoyable.

Architecting this backpacking trip is no different from architecting your life. But what happens most often with people is that they don't architect their life this way. Instead of planning it out, thinking it out, making preparations, asking lots of questions, and having a clear and meaningful destination in mind, *they just go*. They start walking. Wandering aimlessly. Maybe they have some of the right gear on, but not all of it. They might have some of the right supplies for the trip, but don't have everything they need to make it to the end. They don't have a map for the trip. They don't really have any real sense of where they are heading. If you asked them where they are going, they'd say something like, "I'm just gonna go *that* way?" And so they set out on the trip, only to get lost and in need of rescuing, or returning to the starting point, declaring it a failure.

We would call anyone crazy for attempting a backpacking trip this way, but most people *plan their lives just like this*. So, who's crazy after all?

The first step in the Go Next-Level Blueprint is calling a giant time-out and reassessing everything about your life and your business. Before you can begin taking action steps on getting off the plateau and going to new levels, you have to first deeply understand what it is that you want and what you're trying to create. If you ask most people what they want in life, 99 times out of 100 you will get, at best, a very vague answer. "To have a happy and healthy family… To make a ton of money so I can buy anything I want… To make some sort of difference in the lives of others… Only a tiny percentage of the population can answer the question with so much certainty and clarity it inspires everyone who hears it. To Go Next-Level requires us to get master clarity over what it is that we actually want, if we're ever going to achieve it.

Step One in the Go Next-Level Blueprint, just like having clear intentions of the metaphorical backpacking trip, is about having clear intentions for your life and business. This is *the* opportunity, before we start taking action, before we start moving, before we start going in this direction or that direction, to call time-out, and massively start dreaming about what we want.

 Before we can build anything great, we have to know what we are building.

FIRST, WE DREAM

My friend, Chris, called me one day while driving home from one of his construction sites.

CHRIS: "Quentin, you got a minute?"
ME: "Sure, what's going on?", I replied.
CHRIS: "Man, I just need to vent….I am dealing with some customers that are driving me nuts….and I need to figure out how to get them over the finish line with this house…they are never satisfied, want a million changes, and it's nobody's fault but mine".
ME: "They sound like tough customers…but how is it your fault?"
CHRIS: "I should have spent more time with them during design… asking more questions, and the truth is, I should have known better…."

Chris is a custom homebuilder in Nashville, Tennessee. He builds remarkably beautiful homes in the Tennessee countryside. Storybook homes that are works of art. Chris and I chatted on my car ride home that day talking about his business and his frustrations with clients. Wanting to understand his business better and how it caused him frustration, I asked Chris:

"Chris, if someone wants to hire you to build one of your homes, how does the process work? Where do you start with someone?"

Chris explained to me that the first step, and by far the most important and also time-consuming step in the home building process, was the upfront conversations with clients about what they wanted in their house. It wasn't uncommon for Chris to spend months with his clients, and sometimes even years, discussing all of the details about each aspect of the house. Getting into the granular elements like tile colors, square footage of rooms, height of the front door, and what kind of roofing shingles they preferred, were just a few of the many decisions they would need to make together. Chris explained to me that if he didn't get these details fully understood in the very beginning, the project would likely face disaster later in the process. He explained that once construction begins and foundations are set and walls are going up, it's very difficult and sometimes impossible to go backward and make changes.

As Chris was explaining all of this, I couldn't help but think of the incredible parallel between designing lives and businesses, and designing a house. It's exactly the same. We have to know exactly what we want to build, ***before we start building***. This is Step One in the Go Next-Level Blueprint. Before you can create what is right, you have to understand what you really want to create.

ARCHITECTING YOUR IDEAL LIFE WILL FEEL SELFISH

When we start thinking about, and dreaming about, architecting our Ideal Life, we'll run up against some powerful forces, most of which are in our minds. *Before we start thinking about our "dream house", we have to wrestle with some internal demons.* These demons are mostly our personal histories, limiting beliefs, and old narrative stories that keep us stuck on the Early Peak Plateau, and out of range of greater levels of success.

My client Steven, who owns a successful accounting firm, shared with me his vision for his Ideal Life, how he wasn't living it, and how ungratifying his life had become. Steven was at a place in life and business where he had lots of success. He made great money, had a great family, and a great business. On paper, everything in his life seemed perfect. Even though he had achieved so much, it wasn't his Ideal Life. He was on the plateau, and needed to go to his own version of next-level.

When I asked Steven what might be keeping him from pursuing something better for himself, his knee-jerk answer was instant and powerful; "*People are going to be disappointed*".

And that was it for him. The fear of disappointing others was the Achilles heel that was keeping him stuck in the status quo and from going to the next-level. And Steven isn't unique in the slightest. There are millions of people just like him. When any of us start architecting our Ideal Life, we begin leaning into edges of our lives where we realize that in order to pursue something meaningful, it often comes into conflict with other people who might benefit from us living on the plateau. And there's a little voice inside our minds that says…

 "This seems a bit selfish…"

I remember a time when I increased my consulting fees and some of my clients were disappointed. A few were angry with me. And others thought I was greedy. Some simply couldn't afford my new fees and I had to let them go as clients. I understood and empathized with their frustrations, but I made this decision with a lot of contemplation and deliberation. I wrestled with a tremendous amount of guilt and *feeling like I was selfish* for raising my fees. But in the end, I remembered that in order for me to pursue my Ideal

Life, which included a matrix of making more money, seeing fewer clients, and working on things that had more impact, I would have to make some difficult changes. I knew that I would have to fight for my Ideal Life, that it wasn't going to be easy, and it most likely meant letting people down.

 Gut check: You will have to let others down in order to actualize your Ideal Life.

Our culture, societal norms, and the stories in our minds all play a part in keeping us stuck and out of the Ideal Life. We have to wrestle with difficult feelings that present themselves as we make positive changes to our lives that may have a *perceived* negative impact on others. We understand that we can't please everybody and to realize our Ideal Lives, we have to come to a place of acceptance of this reality. But we also need to remember that as some will feel disappointed with our new changes, *many others will rejoice*.

THIS IS THE OPPOSITE OF SELFISH, IT'S YOUR OBLIGATION

In order for us to actualize the talents, gifts, and capabilities God bestowed in us, we have to reframe this inner-narrative that pursuing what is right for you is "selfish". This unhealthy and limiting belief will keep you unhappy, unfulfilled, and living life painfully stuck on the plateau where you're not the best version of yourself. This doesn't serve you, the world, or the people you love the most.

I understand where this inner-narrative and cultural myth comes from though, I really do. We live in a time where selfishness and self-centeredness is a cancer permeating our culture. We live in a time of the narcissistic "selfie" culture where personal happiness trumps the collective greater good.

Crafting your Ideal Life is not the same as selfishness.

So, don't mistake personal *growth* for personal *glory*. There are plenty of people in pursuit of their Ideal Life 365 days a year, growing, and stretching themselves into better versions of themselves. And the world is the beneficiary of them living their Ideal Life. The world is actually in desperate need of you living your Ideal Life. Because when you are living your Ideal Life, you are in the world as the best version of yourself; loving, creative, unique, mission-driven, and full of much to give. There's a huge difference between architecting your Ideal Life and chasing personal happiness at all costs. One is life-giving and one is life-taking. One creates a *win-win* scenario between you and the people you love, and one creates a *win-lose* scenario with you and the people you love. Pursuing your Ideal Life means becoming an even greater asset to your loved ones. Pursuing personal happiness is after the opposite—trying to turn others into 'assets' that serve their personal interests.

 We should feel obligated to give the best version of ourselves to our loved ones around us.

Some people might disagree. In fact, for many, this is a huge gut-check. In their minds, the financial success and material provision they create should be enough … but it isn't. Their wives and children desperately appeal about how all the money in the world can't replace a loving, engaged and present husband & father. And that's because the best thing we can give the world is the Ideal version of ourselves—not money or possessions. Architecting the Ideal Life is creating the healthiest version of you. The version of you filled with joy, vitality, and enthusiasm about life. The people closest to you are the beneficiaries of this new version of you, and this is about as far from selfish as you can get.

Crafting your Ideal Life is stepping out of the small human-sized dreams, and stepping into much larger, God-Sized dreams. It's a faint picture of heaven, only on this side of heaven. When we dig deep in pursuit of our Ideal Life, we'll see how much love we have to give to others, and ourselves. ***This is the opposite of selfishness, this is your obligation.***

Step One in the Go Next-Level Blueprint is your push to design the life you are meant to live. The most honest and true version of yourself coming to life. To not live this life is a disservice to not only yourself, but to humanity around you because we don't get to receive your special talents that only you can offer the world. The average Joe ***doesn't need*** one more average Joe in their lives. He already has thousands of them. What he needs is exposure to someone *different*; someone potent, dynamic and powerful. Someone to admire and emulate, because they model that there's a different way to live beyond playing it safe on the plateau.

Architecting your Ideal Life is not the same as having a midlife crisis, putting a grenade in your life, blowing up your family to run away in your new Ferrari with a twenty-five year old. I can tell you with 100% certainty, that is not your Ideal Life. That is a coping mechanism for suppressed emotional pain. I would even argue that if you don't craft and pursue your Ideal Life, you're more likely to ***actually have an event like this*** in your life. Architecting your Ideal Life is about getting your life back. This is about silencing all the inner voices that tell you what you '*should*' want or desire … and finding out for yourself what truly puts gas in your tank. It's about discovering what you would pursue to the ends of the Earth, simply because you were born for it. That's the only thing worth going after—that thing that ***lights you up***.

You might be reading this and maybe you're hesitant to challenge your current circumstances, or societal norms. Maybe an Ideal Life feels too pie-in-the-sky. Maybe you wonder, "*Is this real? Can I really create something that is Ideal?*" Stay with me and I'll show you exactly how it's more than possible.

GO NEXT-LEVEL PEOPLE HAVE DEFINED THEIR IDEAL LIVES

If you look at the ultra-successful people in the world, and not just financially successful, but successful across all important measurements, you'll notice all of them have a clearly defined Ideal Life. They may use a different term to describe it, but it's the same idea. It's a vision for a future of where they want to go. It's a picture and visual dream they can see and imagine. This picture becomes a guiding light through which all decisions are filtered and choices are made. It clarifies life in such a powerful way that we can ask ourselves *at any given moment*, does making this decision move me closer or further away from my Ideal Life?

Only a tiny fragment of the population has taken the time to actually sit down and construct their Ideal Life. There are many reasons why people might not do this, which we'll discuss later. However, without a clearly articulated and well-defined future picture of where you want to go, you'll never get there. Without a map, you'll never reach your destination. Without a Blueprint, you'll never get the house right. And without a clearly defined Ideal Life, you won't build the life and business of your dreams.

 If you want to go to the next level, you better know where you're headed.

And we can't shortcut the process either. We can't just borrow someone else's Ideal Life and try to mimic it. That won't work. We have to take the time to create our own. In order for your Ideal Life to make sense and be a congruent guiding force, it has to incorporate your background, upbringing, influences, joys, sorrows, personality type, and so on. There's no getting around this one. Either you take ownership and design *your* Ideal Life, or *one will be chosen for you at random*, by people and forces external to you.

In a study of 233 millionaires in the United States, Tom Corely, author of "Rich Habits", concluded that a common denominator trait of the ultra-wealthy is they were *extremely focused on* **what mattered most** *to them*. When we look at successful people, we need to remember that success leaves clues.

 Architecting your Ideal Life is about getting focused on what matters most to you.

IF YOU CAN'T DREAM IT, YOU CAN'T CREATE IT

To begin architecting your Ideal Life, you have to spend time in contemplation and introspection, getting your brain thinking about, dreaming about, and reflecting on what you really want. Remember, like the example I used with my friend Chris the homebuilder, we have to spend the necessary up-front time thinking about the house we want to build before we start construction. Too many people start building their lives, only to find out down the road they were building something they actually didn't want.

GO NEXT-LEVEL ACTION STEP:

On the next page you will find some questions to help you as you begin this process. Before reading the rest of this chapter, grab your journal, and actually write down your answers to these questions. Don't just go through it as a cognitive exercise. Actually write your answers. When you force yourself to answer the questions in writing, the answers move you one step closer to being real.

20 Questions for Architecting Your Ideal Life:

1. How do I want to spend my time in my Ideal Life?
2. What does my perfect day look like in my Ideal Life?
3. Imagine your Ideal Life in six quadrants of a pie chart; what categories are most important to fill that pie chart?
4. How do I want to spend my time at work in my Ideal Life?
5. What specific tasks am I doing in my Ideal Life to make money?
6. How much money do I want to make in my Ideal Life?
7. Who am I serving in my Ideal Life?
8. What kind of things do I want to spend my money on in my Ideal Life?
9. How many hours do I want to work per week in my Ideal Life?
10. Imagine your Ideal Life *at work* in three quadrants of a pie chart; what categories are most important to you to fill that pie chart?
11. If you had to pick one role model of an Ideal Life, who is that and why?
12. What do I do for fun in my Ideal Life?
13. What unique dent in the universe do I make in my Ideal Life?
14. What kind of relationships do I want to have in my Ideal Life?
15. What important hobbies do I want to master in my Ideal Life?
16. Where do I want to live in my Ideal Life?
17. How will the world be a better place in my Ideal Life?
18. What am I creating in my Ideal Life?
19. What do I want to be remembered for in my Ideal Life?
20. What will my legacy be in my Ideal Life?

RECOGNIZE THE FEAR, AND KEEP MOVING

As quick as the excitement about answering these questions comes, *fear* will also pop into your mind and remind you to play it safe. *"Don't do this, you're crazy!" "Everything is fine just as it is, you don't need to rock the boat." "You're not going to live your Ideal Life anyway so why get so worked up about it?"* Our brains are wired for self-preservation and we talk ourselves out of intimidating and challenging things, even if we know it's ultimately a better choice and what we want. Thinking through these questions feels risky. There is a reason, after all, that most people don't live an Ideal Life. In order for us to achieve an Ideal Life, we have to **become friends with the fears** that also keep us from an Ideal Life. These fears, which become hurdles, are what will keep you from creating your Ideal Life—so let's take a look at them:

THE FIVE MOST COMMON HURDLES STOPPING YOU FROM ARCHITECTING AN IDEAL LIFE:

1. You are worried others will judge you for pursuing your Ideal Life.
2. You are worried others will be disappointed in you for pursuing your Ideal Life.
3. You are worried that you may fail in pursuing your Ideal Life.
4. You are worried that it's all too much and too overwhelming pursuing your Ideal Life.
5. You are worried that pursuing your Ideal Life is selfish.

These fears are normal and expectable. The strongest and most influential part of our brain is far more concerned with self-preservation via an **emotional flight response** than dreaming about an Ideal Life. Dreaming can feel scary. But that is OK, we can be aware of that part of our brain, make peace with it, and override it. Because there is another part of our brain, though it is much smaller and less vocal, that wants us to find joy, fulfillment, and a zeal for living again that only pursuing what our Ideal Life can provide. We can exercise this part of our brain too, and it can have just as strong an influence over our decisions and behavior. It's up to us to train that part of our brain too.

THE TYRANNY OF THE URGENT

Sometimes the hardest thing to do in life is call time-out and reassess. We fear that if we don't keep moving and keep being "productive" things will fall apart. Or worse, we fear that if we stop and do deep self-reflection, we might be honest and discover things about what we want that bring up fear inside. We may not like how we feel when we slow down for a minute and dream about where we're at in life and where we want to be, but it's essential to make time for this. There is a simple formula for success and achievement and it goes like this:

STEP #1: PLAN
STEP #2: EXECUTE
STEP #3: REEVALUATE
STEP #4: REPEAT

I'm not exactly sure where you are reading this book, but I know many people are great at executing and staying busy, but not so great at the **planning** stage when it comes to dreaming about the Ideal Life you want to build. We may be decent at planning this week or this month, but not so great about deeply thinking where we want to go in the next ten years, and creating a map to get there. In some instances, ***busyness can be a form of laziness***, because planning and dreaming is the real work you're avoiding. You're putting off the harder work by using busyness as an avoidance distraction. Other people might even buy it, but deep down, you know it's not getting you where you want to go.

Step One in the Go Next-Level Blueprint forces you to call time-out to begin architecting the long-term vision for your life. If you want to achieve more, get unstuck from any plateaus, it starts with the creation of an Ideal Life as a concept. You'll achieve at most a fraction of what *you're really capable of* without a compelling vision for an Ideal Life.

RE-EARTHING OLD DREAMS

When we put pen to paper and craft an Ideal Life, it changes us. There's something powerful that happens when we take thoughts that only reside in our minds and put them on paper. I've seen this truth in action. I was speaking to a group of real estate professionals in Orlando Florida and a guy named Dave in the audience was writing his Ideal Life Statement. During the exercise, Dave wrote that he would "*drive a nice car*" in his Ideal Life. When I questioned him about what he meant by a nice car, he said, "*A Porsche*".

I said, "*Whoa, that is a nice car. What kind of Porsche do you want?*" With lots of hesitation and reluctance to answer the question, he finally said in a quiet voice hoping too many people didn't hear him, "*A 911 Turbo*".

I said back to him, "*I love it! Those are expensive....around $200K, I believe?*"

Dave replied back to me with a nervous chuckle, "*I couldn't imagine ever getting that car*".

I responded to Dave matter of factly, "*I know you could get that car, and if it matters to you, you will get that car*".

I got to know Dave better throughout that event and he shared that ever since he was a little kid, he was a fan of 911's and dreamed about owning one, one day. He said he had posters of 911's on his bedroom wall growing up, but as he got older and life clicked on, he slowly resigned himself to giving up on that dream. But as much as he'd have liked to give up on the dream, it was still deep inside him. He still yearned for that car.

I insisted Dave change the wording on his Ideal Life Statement narration from "*a nice car*" to a "*911 Turbo*". Now he had something to go after. Now he was being honest with himself about his dreams. Now it was simply about following the other steps in the Blueprint to help him get to this dream. You see, we all are like Dave. We all have had dreams we let die. We were all little kids at some point who had wild and big dreams, but we didn't know how to reach them, so we let them die. Step One in getting off the Early Peak Plateau is about re-earthing those old dreams.

LET'S BE AUDACIOUS IN OUR DREAMING

For us to reach optimal levels of success, we have to be driven by a picture of an Ideal Life that motivates us to take action, and do the hard work, so we can achieve what we really want in life. And although Dave's story was about that special Porsche, crafting the Ideal Life is so much bigger than what we want from a material perspective. Maybe for you, it's not about the car you've always dreamed of. Maybe that's not important to you. Maybe for you, architecting your Ideal Life is about the Ideal in your family situation, returning to joy and fun, your health, taking exciting risks, or pursuing your mission in life. It's the complete picture of our lives that we *declare* to be our Ideal situation. And this picture of the future becomes our driving force and propels us forward.

For most of the world, people are simply going through the motions. Not in pursuit of their Ideal, they live lives that feel empty, unfulfilling, or at best, moderately getting by. This is no way to live. They do day to day tasks they dislike, are in relationships with people that are ungratifying, and don't really have a greater sense of mission in life. The starting place for all of us is to simply call time-out. Spend time really thinking about what we want. And to not be afraid to be audacious in our dreaming.

The good news is you have complete control and ownership of that *one* person who can stop you. He or she is not hard to find. Pull out your driver's license and look at the person in the photo, because that's the culprit. You are your toughest opponent ... and well, guess what? If you win these battles, you will be creating a new future and able to fulfill what you really want. This isn't the time to play it safe. Really go for it. Don't spend even one more minute second guessing yourself. Do the work and launch yourself toward creating that picture of your Ideal Life.

GO NEXT-LEVEL ACTION STEP:

Now, it's time to return to your journal and begin writing out your Ideal Life statement. Don't keep reading until you write this out. Use the template below to fill in the blanks and architect your own compelling vision for your future. Remember, really go for it. Now isn't the time to play it small and safe.

GO NEXT-LEVEL IDEAL LIFE STATEMENT

In the Ideal Life I'm living, I'll spend the majority of my time being _____ , learning _____ , maximizing _____ , having _____ , and helping _____ .
For work, I _____ regularly.
Most of my time at work will be spent _____ , and _____ .
In my Ideal Life, I'll work _____ hours per week doing exactly what I love. In my Ideal Life, I will generate _____ per year in annual income, which will allow me a fully rewarding lifestyle.

This income will allow me to _____ , _____ , and _____ .
The first thing I will buy when I reach this income level will be _____ .
In my Ideal Life, I'll spend more time on the things I love; my passions and hobbies like _____ , _____ , and _____ .

In my Ideal life, my most important relationships will feel _____ , _____ , and _____ .
In my Ideal Life, I want to spend more time doing _____ with _____ .

And at the end of my life, the legacy I will be remembered for will be _____ , and as a person who _____ .

At my funeral, people will say how positively _____ I was, and people will gather in celebration of my life.

GO NEXT-LEVEL KEY-TAKEAWAYS

CHAPTER ONE: "What Do You Want?"

→ The first step in the Go Next-Level Blueprint is calling a giant time-out and reassessing everything about your life and your business. Before you can begin taking action steps on getting off the plateau and going to new levels, you have to first deeply understand **what it is that you want and what you're trying to create**.

→ Before we can build anything great, we have to know what we are building.

→ When we start thinking about, and dreaming about, architecting our **Ideal Life**, we'll run up against some powerful forces, most of which are in our minds. Before we start thinking about our "dream house", we have to wrestle with some internal demons. These demons are mostly our personal histories, limiting beliefs, and old narrative stories that keep us stuck on the Early Peak Plateau, and out of range of greater levels of success.

→ You will have to **let others down** in order to actualize your Ideal Life. We understand that we can't please everybody and to realize our Ideal Lives, we have to come to a place of acceptance of this reality. But we also need to remember that as some will feel disappointed with our new changes, **many others will rejoice**.

→ In order for us to achieve an Ideal Life, we have to become friends with the fears that also keep us from an Ideal Life. These fears, which become hurdles, are what will keep you from creating your Ideal Life.

→ The world is actually in desperate need of you living your Ideal Life. Because when you are living your Ideal Life, you are in the world as the best version of yourself; loving, creative, unique, mission-driven, and full of much to give. There's a huge difference between architecting your Ideal Life and chasing personal happiness at all costs. **One is life-giving and one is life-taking.**

→ Crafting your Ideal Life is stepping out of the small human-sized dreams, and stepping into much larger, God-Sized dreams. It's a faint picture of heaven, only on this side of heaven. We should feel obligated to give the best version of ourselves to our loved ones around us.

→ Step One in the Go Next-Level Blueprint is your push to design the life you are meant to live. The most **honest and true** version of yourself coming to life. To not live this life is a disservice to not only yourself, but to humanity around you because we don't get to receive your special talents that only you can offer the world.

→ If you look at the ultra-successful people in the world, and not just financially successful, but successful across all important measurements, you'll notice all of them have a clearly defined Ideal Life. If you want to go to the next level, you better know where you're headed.

CHAPTER TWO

WHY DO YOU WANT IT?

GO NEXT-LEVEL BLUEPRINT STEP #2:
KNOWING WHAT BREAKS YOUR HEART AND WHAT PISSES YOU OFF

> When a person can't find a deep sense of meaning, they distract themselves with pleasure.
>
> VIKTOR FRANKL

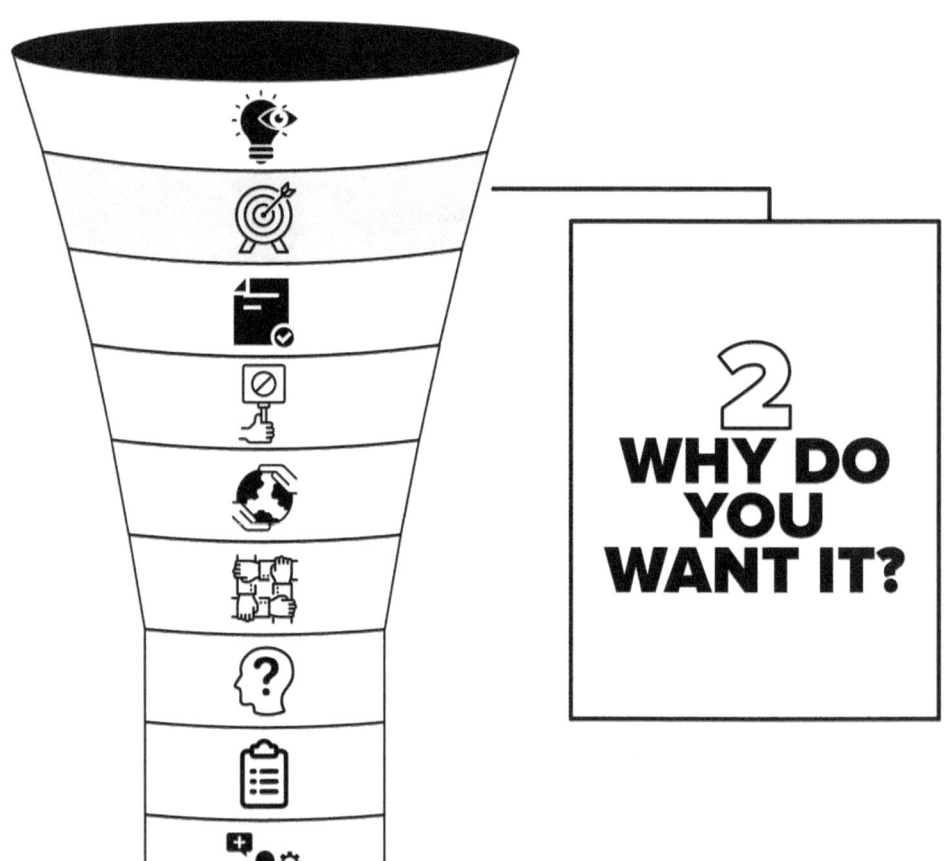

CLARITY OF PURPOSE BECOMES AN ACCELERATOR

In order to launch to the next level and fulfill everything you want in life and business, you have to discover your purpose, or what we'll call your Big Why. Your Big Why is a declaration of clarity on the unique purpose you have on this earth. You, yes you reading this, you are unique, with a special set of attributes, desires, history, and experiences unlike anyone else. No one else is like you. When you develop this clarity of purpose, it will become your accelerator, that you've likely been missing, that will help you break past the Early Peak Plateau and launch to new levels.

You might think you don't have a unique purpose because *"I'm just an accountant"*, or *"I'm just a real estate agent"*, but that isn't true. Your occupation may be shared by a million other people, but what is not shared by anyone, let alone millions of others, is your personal uniqueness. Nowhere on this planet can you find another CPA or teacher who has lived a life of experiences and memories identical to yours. Nowhere is there someone who does what you do for a living, and who also sees with a perspective identical to yours. What deeply matters to you is not the same as what deeply matters to your colleague.

The lie, that "I am just a(an) _____" is what keeps people stuck in the status of *good enough* and on the plateau. If you want to reach for greatness, if you want to really go high level, you have to get clear on, and begin actively living out, your unique purpose. Your unique purpose, your "Big Why", is the driving force that propels you to tackle each day as it becomes the intrinsic motivation that gets you out of bed and ready to move mountains. It's an ***energy*** that is driven by something deep inside you. It is power. It's the Spirit of God inside of you.

Now, before we go one step further, let's address an elephant in the room; If concepts like *purpose*, and *Big Why's* feel complex, cosmic, and esoteric, you're not alone, they can be overly complicated. They can be difficult to practically wrap our heads around. But they don't have to be and they are often unnecessarily confusing. So let's make it straightforward.

When I was first introduced to the idea of getting clear on my purpose, I was resistant to the idea because it sounded very ethereal and vague; like it was some spiritual woo-woo idea that was hard to grab onto. But the truth is, it's none of those things. Getting clear on your purpose is as easy as understanding three important truths:

1. You have limited time on this earth.
2. You are unique with different experiences, attributes, and perspectives.
3. You want to accomplish something important.

If you agree with these three statements and take them to heart, then you will unlock your Big Why. **Your Big Why is at the center of these three truths.**

PURPOSE ELIMINATES BURNOUT

In order for us to achieve the Ideal Life that we crafted in Chapter One, we need a deep motivation and a driving force that pushes us forward. What is going to cause you to wake up early, work hard, sacrifice, and do what's necessary to pursue your Ideal Life? The answer lies in discovering your Big Why. When you gain clarity on your Big Why, it's nearly impossible to not pursue it because it's so personally meaningful and compellingly powerful. And when your Big Why is pursued with tenacity, your movement off the plateau onto your next level becomes an outcome and unintended positive consequence.

> *"Singleness of purpose is one of the chief essentials for success in life, no matter what may be one's aim."*
>
> **JOHN D. ROCKEFELLER**

Burnout isn't real. Or at least, how we typically think of it is wrong.

Burnout is just the feeling we get when we're not in alignment with our purpose. Too many people are working hard on the wrong things. They may be exhausted, stressed out, and on their last legs at work, but it isn't because they're just working too many hours or have a bad work-life balance ratio, it's because they're working on the wrong things. Whenever I meet someone who's struggling with *burnout*, within minutes I'll discover they have no compelling Big Why. You can spend your whole life trying to fight against burnout, incorporating superficial "work-life balance" methods, or you can develop a compelling Big Why and eliminate all of these things entirely. When you're clear on your Big Why and you're working toward something rich in meaning and fulfillment, burnout doesn't exist.

Having a clear Big Why that we're relentlessly in pursuit of, gives us extraordinarily high levels of motivation and we're able to achieve the most audacious goals. We remain faithfully committed to even the most mundane tasks. It's not that we become superheroes, but as our perspective shifts around our purpose, we develop uncanny stamina to do what can seem very superhero'ish.

Many people are stuck on Early Peak Plateaus and not fulfilling what they want because they don't have a clear and compelling understanding of their purpose. People without a clear purpose are going through the motions; waking up, working hard, but deep inside they are dissatisfied, feeling what they think is burnout, and wondering, "Is this all there is?" If you've felt this way, clarity of purpose is the rope ladder that will take you to the next level.

GREATNESS ONLY FLOWS FROM A COMPELLING "WHY"

> *A life devoted to things is a dead life, a stump;*
> *a God-shaped life is a flourishing tree.*
>
> **PROVERBS 11:28 (MSG)**

In order for us to Go Next-Level and achieve maximum levels of success and significance, whatever that definition is to us, we have to have a fire in our bellies that drives us for more. This deep motivation grows into a raging fire compelling us to wake up early, put in those extra hours, and go the extra mile. When we're driven by something so powerful, we'll move to extraordinary levels. When we're not driven by something this powerful, we'll be on the fast track to burnout. This *"thing"* that drives us is our Big Why.

I was a finance major in college and I spent the first part of my career working in real estate private equity. I had a great career in a prestigious role. By all accounts, I was doing exceedingly well and was on the exact right path. I was "living the dream". So everyone who looked at my life would have assumed from the outside, and so I tried to convince myself on the inside.

But the truth is, I didn't enjoy any of it. I loathed going to work and dreaded having to do one more client meeting at a fancy hotel. At the time, I could never understand why I disliked my career so much. It didn't seem rational. I had a "great job" by most people's standards. I felt bad for feeling bad and told myself to work harder, suck it up, and just get over it. I beat myself up for not being grateful and pushed really hard to remind myself of "all the good things" I had. No matter how much I tried to force gratitude, I languished in discontent. I couldn't stop wondering why I was so unhappy.

So, I just kept showing up, keeping my head down, working harder and harder for that next bonus, because I thought, "Well maybe this is what will make me happy?" I tried to be appreciative, but none of those mental tricks made things better. Having no understanding of the power of purpose at the time, I just tried to keep moving forward and push all of those feelings of dread aside. Eventually, stuck on my own plateau, I reached a breaking point. Feeling like I was breathing underwater, I knew of no other decision than to quit my job. I had to get out of the arena causing me so much suffering.

Looking back, I know now the problem wasn't with my job. There was nothing inherently wrong with my career. The problem was deeper than that, and the problem was inside of me.

The problem wasn't the job. The problem was that I wasn't clear on my purpose. And it haunted me.

 Does any of this resonate with you?

What I didn't know then that I know so clearly now is this: If you want to achieve great levels of success for the **long run** and get launched off any stuck plateaus, it's essential you are clear about your Big Why. The very thing I didn't have.

A WARNING ABOUT PURSUING YOUR PURPOSE
When it comes to pursuing the very things that deeply matter to you, you have to be prepared for the world, and sometimes even the people you love, to not be supportive. And sometimes even worse than being non-supportive, you might even find these same people actively working against you.

But why? Why do people actively work against us pursuing what is most meaningful to us?

There are lots of reasons. They might fear you'll fail and get hurt. They might be envious because you're taking a chance on yourself. They might feel insecure about their own lack of purpose. They might fear you'll leave them behind. Or it might be some combination of these.

When you start pursuing purposeful things, most of the world will want you to be less grandiose and they will tell you to be more practical and just buckle down and *"get a job"*. That *"no one"* really gets to pursue their purpose, and that pursuing your purpose is reckless. Now sometimes, sure, we need to make short term less-purposeful sacrifices for the pursuit of our long-term Big Why. This is part of the natural growth process. But never believe any cultural lies that tell you that you can't pursue your personal purpose on earth.

 Anyone that discourages you from pursuing your purpose doesn't have a purpose themselves.

The general messaging from others is going to be some version of telling you to *"play it safe"*, but I say **playing it safe is discovering your unique purpose and pursuing it**. Because to live a life out of alignment with your purpose, is to live a life stuck on plateaus, apathy, and unfulfillment, and that is to no benefit to anyone else around, including yourself.

In order for us to go to the next level, we have to understand that **we'll never get there** without pursuing our greater purpose, and in pursuing this worthy endeavor, not everyone is going to be your raving fan.

THE COST OF NOT LIVING YOUR PURPOSE

Many professional athletes hate their jobs. It's a little-known secret that many of the highest paid people in the world are surprisingly miserable. You'd think with all the money, the fame, and "doing what they love", they'd be on the top of the world, but most are not. I've coached several professional athletes over the years, and access to behind the veil of professional sports has shown me it's not all that it's cracked up to be. One of my clients, Steve, drafted in the first round out of college, played in the NFL for eleven years. Steve was very talented. But what very few people knew about Steve is that he actually hated playing football, and would suffer from debilitating panic attacks before every game and every practice for eleven straight years.

His teammates chalked it up to pre-game nerves and anxiety, but it was much more complicated than that. It was deeper. Steve had to force himself to play this role. Not aligned with his purpose, every game and every practice was forcing a square peg into a round hole. He detested every minute of being a professional athlete.

 Playing football wasn't his purpose.

But the golden handcuffs and the lifestyle he became accustomed to made it very difficult to walk away. And what made it even worse, whenever he tried to talk about it, no one could really understand why he didn't like playing football. He barely understood it himself. After all, he had achieved what is celebrated in our culture as reaching the pinnacle of life. Making millions of dollars... Achieving celebrity status... Playing a sport at the highest level...

But making millions, being a celebrity, and playing a sport at the highest level means very little if it's not in alignment with purpose. Ancient wisdom and mountains of research teach us that more money, at the expense of doing what we have been put on the earth to do, brings very little fulfillment.

What Steve intuitively knew about himself at the deepest level, but was too afraid to admit, was that he wasn't supposed to be in the NFL. Despite his natural athleticism, sporting accolades, and everyone else's belief in him as an athlete, he was totally out of alignment with his purpose, and he was paying a heavy emotional, psychological, and spiritual toll. He was stuck on his own plateau.

EVERYONE HAS A PURPOSE, BUT VERY FEW KNOW WHAT IT IS

So let me ask you a few questions to get you thinking about your own clearly defined purpose and compelling Big Why. Remember, if we want to go to the next level and fulfill everything we want, we have to know *why* we're waking up every morning and doing what we're doing. Without the deep conviction our Big Why carries, we will remain stuck on that painful plateau and unable to Go Next-Level.

GO NEXT-LEVEL ACTION STEP:

Now, I want you to grab your pen and journal and work through these questions below. Remember, it's essential that you actually answer the questions. Write something down. Write down the first thing that comes to your mind without overthinking it. Then, after you've written it down, go back and ponder, contemplate, and spend more time thinking about the questions. But don't read past this section without writing something down.

- If nothing changes in my life, what will I regret on my deathbed?
- What pisses me off?
- What makes me come alive?
- What breaks my heart?
- What do I do that makes me forget to eat?
- What contributions do I want to make in my life?
- If money were no concern, how would I spend my time?
- Where do I most enjoy spending my time?
- What do I need to do that embarrasses me more?
- What's true about me today that would make my seven-year-old self cry?

Having a purpose is not some spiritual woo-woo thing. It's simply answering this question:

 How do I want to spend my limited time in a way that is meaningfully important to me?

WHY DO YOU EXIST?

It's time to light a fire in your belly. In Chapter One, we're asking, "*What Do You Want*"? We talked about architecting a Big Dream; the Ideal Life that we want to create for ourselves. It's that picture and a vision of what we're looking at five, ten, or twenty years from now that gets us excited. In this chapter, we're asking, "*Why Do You Want It?*" We're talking about the Big Why; which is the deep conviction around purpose that drives us toward launching off any of the places we feel plateaued. Without a deeply convicted and compelling purpose for our lives, we won't be able to sustain the climb required to Go Next-Level.

As I write this book now, I have a clear picture of people I know who are living well below their capacity for greatness. This book is written for them, and the millions of others in the world who painfully settle for so much less than what they are capable of in all areas of their lives. This book is written to my younger self who knew nothing about the concept of purpose. I want more for you—for your sake, and for the world's sake that needs your gifts and talents.

 Remember, it's not enough to know what you want; we also have to know why we want it.

Do you want to know what pisses me off? Do you want to know what breaks my heart? Seeing the possibilities and untapped potential in people who settle for so much less than God has designed them for. That is my motivation to do what I do. That is my Big Why and that is enough for me to wake up early every morning, prioritize what matters most, and put these words on paper.

 So what is that for you? What is that thing that pisses you off, and breaks your heart?

Here are some real-life examples of Big Why statements taken from participants at one of my workshops. Take a guess at which one is mine:

"*My Big Why is to inspire every person I meet to become a better parent.*"
"*My Big Why is to change the world with new technology.*"
"*My Big Why is to ignite passion into people who have forgotten what they are capable of.*"
"*My Big Why is to inspire the artful creativity in others.*"
"*My Big Why is to provide underprivileged children with more learning opportunities.*"

You can see how different Big Why statements will vary from person to person. There is **only one** Big Why statement listed above that will make me get out of bed early in the morning and grind. And that one is mine. None of the other statements get me excited, and they're not supposed to—because they're not mine. All of these are great Big Why statements, but only one of them has my fingerprints.

Only **our own** Big Why will work to keep us committed, motivated, and reaching all of our massive goals.

WE'LL LIKELY FIND OUR BIG WHY IN THE DAY-TO-DAY

My friend Scott owns a mid-size IT company in Des Moines, Iowa with about twenty employees. Scott had always been a geeky tech guy and loved computers from the time he was little. He built his first computer when he was eight with his Dad, who was also an early adopter of computers and technology in the 1980's. As a little boy, Scott developed a love for soldering parts of motherboards, and diving deep into the parts of computer technology that most of us mere mortals couldn't comprehend. After college, Scott started his own IT business focused on IT support for other small companies in the Des Moines, Iowa area. By the time Scott was forty-five, he had built his business to the point where he was mostly out of the day-to-day operations, and larger IT companies were looking to purchase his business. A huge success by most measurements.

One day, Scott and I were having dinner and I asked Scott about his business. He told me about how unhappy he was and how much this business had "taken the life out of him". He explained to me that at the first decent offer to sell his business, he was going to take it, with no clear plans of what to do next. He just wanted to get off the bus at the next possible stop.

Through a long series of back and forth over a three-hour dinner that night, I asked Scott about the last time he felt a real sense of fulfillment in his business. I asked him when he last felt a sense of passion for what he was doing.

In a moment that seemed completely out of the blue I asked Scott to tell me, *"What really pisses you off? What breaks your heart?"*

At first confused, but with a little reflection, Scott described an experience he had about four years prior when he helped a small family-owned business recover intellectual property that had been used as ransom in a cyber security attack. Scott and his team helped the family recover what was rightfully theirs, get their business back up and running, and create a new system of protective structures for the family business so this wouldn't happen again.

As Scott told this story, I witnessed his posture change. I saw him come alive, become energetic, and I could see the passion he felt as he, without knowing, was touching on the edges of his Big Why. He described this situation as if he was protecting the small kid on the third grade playground from getting bullied. There was power, and anger, and passion in his voice when he told the story. Using his business expertise, his technical skills, and his passion for helping the little guy fight the Goliath's of cyber security, this is what made Scott come alive.

Toward the end of conversation that night, I asked Scott what turned into a life-changing question for him: Would you keep your business if you could only do the kind of work where you're helping the little guy fight the Goliath's? He said, "Yes, I would keep it, without question."

 A fundamental truth inside all Big Why's: Your purpose will always be found in service to someone or something outside of yourself.

And that was it. Scott needed to change his business model to serve his purpose. The old model made money, but it didn't serve his Big Why. The new model made money *and* served his Big Why. As of the release of this book, Scott's company with the new business model has grown exponentially and pivoted primarily into doing cyber-security work for small business owners. Scott is living on purpose.

Prior to this conversation, Scott had all the pieces of success, except one. He had stability, financial security, freedom, plenty of money, and a legacy, but he didn't have a compelling Big Why that drove him. All of the success and money weren't enough to sustain him and keep him going. He had to have something deeper—this is the Big Why. Scott didn't need to go become a monk or have some mountaintop experience to discover his Big Why—with some tweaking and changing, he could find it right in the middle of where he already was—in the day-to-day of his existing business.

Scott, like most of us, had a Big Why that was very close to where he already existed, but he missed it in the details.

SUPERCHARGE YOUR LIFE WITH A BIG WHY

Without a Big Why, we can do some things well, but we'll never reach the true Go Next-Level potential. The Big Why is like the turbo boosters on the jet that will launch you off the plateau. Jets can't fly without them.

Declaring your Big Why will supercharge your life with the power of purpose.

When we go through life without a convincing Big Why, we're at risk for an acceptance of a mediocre "good enough". On the surface, the "good enough" level doesn't seem *that bad*. We can get married, have a family, work a stable job and maybe retire someday with a "good enough" approach. But you never really know the pain of regret involved in the "good enough" approach until you get toward the finish line. You'll reach some point in your life and you start to question the "good enough" approach. You might have everything you thought you wanted, but you're not fulfilled. You're not satisfied. And something aches in your soul because you haven't lived the life you were called to live. You haven't pursued your passion. And this is why millions of people are stuck on the plateau and unable to Go Next-Level.

In Chapter One, we talked about getting clear with what you want. In this Chapter, we're getting clear with *why you want it*; which is found in discovering your Big Why.

And wherever you're at reading this, it's never too late to begin to discover your Big Why.

If you feel that nagging ache inside of yourself wondering if you've lived to your fullest potential, that is an invitation to get clarity on your Big Why. It's a prerequisite for getting unstuck and fulfilling everything you want in life and business.

GO NEXT-LEVEL ACTION STEP:

So, I'll ask you again even more directly; what is your Big Why? Using your answers to the questions in the previous section, brainstorm four versions of your own unique Big Why statement. Once completed, you will refer to it often on your success journey to Go Next-Level. It will remind you of why you're doing what you're doing and why it really matters. We need these reminders because it's too easy to become distracted by the demands of life and get off course. Your Big Why statement serves as an anchor to help you stay committed to what's most important to you, meet all of your massive goals, and helps you stay motivated when you need a little push.

Don't go on to Chapter Three until you've written four versions of your Big Why statement. Remember, you don't have to get it perfect, you just have to get started. Review back to the examples I provided in this chapter to help give you structure, and also refer back to the questions you answered earlier in the chapter to give you clarity about what is most essential to you.

MY BIG WHY IS TO: _____

_____

_____

_____

MY BIG WHY IS TO: _____

_____

_____

_____

MY BIG WHY IS TO: _____

_____

_____

_____

MY BIG WHY IS TO: _____

_____

_____

_____

GO NEXT-LEVEL KEY-TAKEAWAYS

CHAPTER TWO: "Why Do You Want It?"

→ In order to launch to the next level and fulfill everything you want in life and business, you have to **discover your purpose,** or what we'll call your Big Why. Your Big Why is a declaration of clarity on the unique purpose you have on this earth.

→ You might think you don't have a unique purpose because "I'm just an accountant", or "I'm just a real estate agent", but that isn't true. Your occupation may be shared by a million other people, but what is not shared by anyone, let alone millions of others, is your personal uniqueness.

→ Your unique purpose, your "Big Why", is the driving force that **propels you to tackle each day** as it becomes the intrinsic motivation that gets you out of bed and ready to move mountains. It's an energy that is driven by something deep inside you.

→ Getting clear on your purpose is as easy as understanding **three important truths:**

1. You have limited time on this earth.
2. You are unique with different experiences, attributes, and perspectives.
3. You want to accomplish something important.

→ If you agree with these three statements and take them to heart, then you will unlock your Big Why. Your Big Why is at the **center of these three truths.**

→ Burnout is just the feeling we get when we're not in alignment with our purpose. Too many people are working hard on the wrong things. They may be exhausted, stressed out, and on their last legs at work, but it isn't because they're just working too many hours or have a bad work-life balance ratio, it's because they're working on the wrong things.

→ You can spend your whole life trying to fight against burnout, incorporating superficial "work-life balance" methods, or you can develop a compelling Big Why and eliminate all of these things entirely. When you're clear on your Big Why and you're working toward something rich in meaning and fulfillment, **burnout doesn't exist.**

→ When it comes to pursuing the very things that deeply matter to you, you have to be prepared for the world, and sometimes even the people you love, to not be supportive. And sometimes even worse than being non-supportive, you might even find these same people actively working against you. Anyone that discourages you from pursuing your purpose doesn't have a purpose themselves.

→ Having a purpose is not some spiritual woo-woo thing. It's simply answering this question:

> » *How do I want to spend my limited time in a way that is meaningfully important to me?*

→ A fundamental truth inside all Big Why's: Your purpose will always be found **in service to someone or something outside of yourself**.

→ Without a Big Why, we can do some things well, but we'll never reach the true Go Next-Level potential. The Big Why is like the **turbo boosters** on the jet that will launch you off the plateau. Jets can't fly without them. Declaring your Big Why will supercharge your life with the power of purpose.

CHAPTER THREE

WHAT DO YOU NEED TO SAY "YES" TO?

GO NEXT-LEVEL BLUEPRINT STEP #3:
BECOMING A GO NEXT-LEVEL RISK-TAKER

> There is no achievement without failure.
>
> JOHN MAXWELL

THE *Go Next-Level* BLUEPRINT

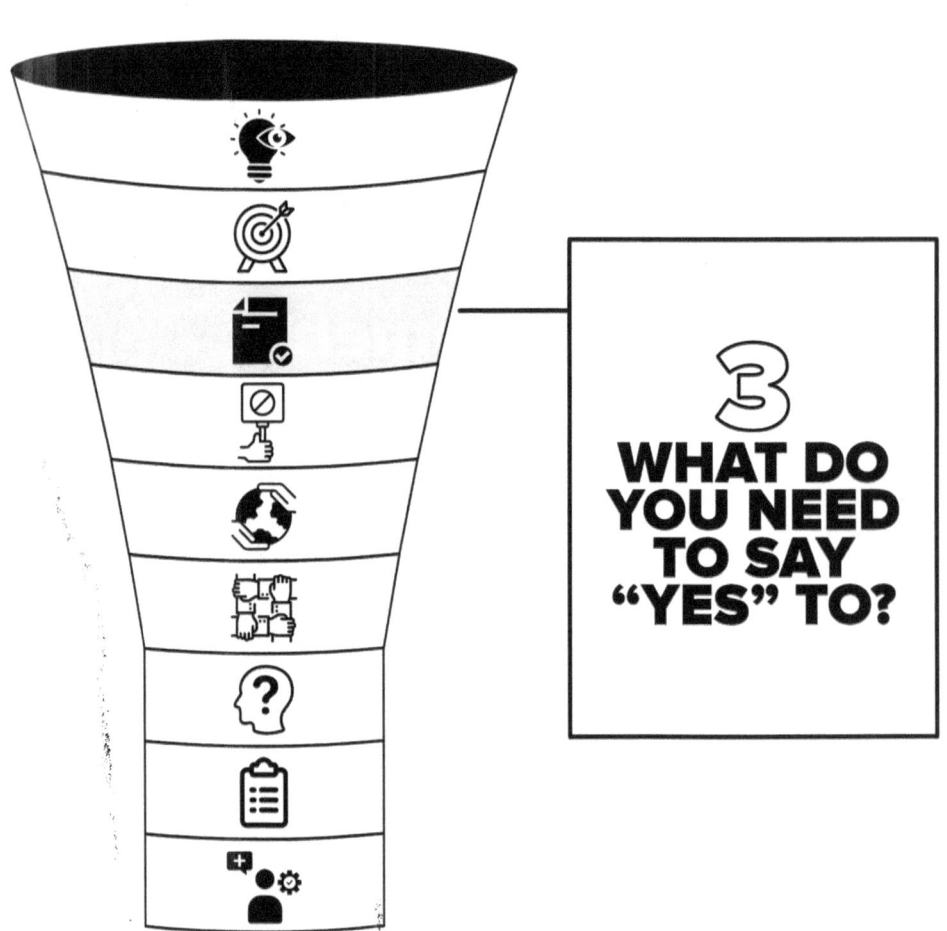

RISKING YOUR WAY OFF THE PLATEAU

Reaching something great requires that we take chances. And to Go Next-Level and get unstuck from any plateaus, it requires us to take the kinds of chances that we're scared to take. As counter-intuitive as it may seem, a truism about people who have gone to the next level and launched off the Early Peak Plateau is that they have become masters in risk-taking and also failure. Go Next-Level people do not like to fail, but they are not afraid to fail. The difference between going to the next level and remaining stuck on the plateau will be your perspective on risk-taking and how you perceive the possibility of failure. You're reading this book because you desire something more; you want to Go Next-Level. To get there, you have to make friends with the discomfort of taking chances, and stretch yourself into someone that reimagines the possibilities of failures.

 It is only with risk-taking, and making peace with failing, that you'll ever achieve your wildest dreams and get unstuck from your plateau.

When we first look at people who have built great lives and gone to the next level in life or business, what we see on the surface is all of the outward success. We see them living optimal lives. What we don't see are the thousands of failures, setbacks, and calculated risks that laid the path for them to get to their own version of greatness. We don't see all of the sleepless nights they experienced; looking foolish and being perceived by others as a failure. But they certainly experienced it. The only difference between these people and people who stay stuck on the Early Peak Plateau is they didn't let these fears stop them. They understand that taking risks is necessary to get them to the next level of where they want to go, and they embrace all the discomfort that comes with risk-taking as part of that journey.

To Go Next-Level, we have to *start saying "yes"* to taking more risks.

Because it is only in-and-through taking chances, *and no other way*, that will get you off the stuck plateau. People get stuck on the plateau because they stopped taking chances. And they stopped taking chances because they became afraid to fail. So, it is only when you embrace the reality that taking chances often produces failures, and failures *are* the gateway to pass through on your way to greater levels of success. It's time to embrace this reality. When you spend your life avoiding appropriate risk-taking because you don't want to fail, you'll never get to the next level.

This is the irony about success and fulfillment; success *only* and *always* follows some type of potential calculated risk, set back, or doing something that could result in failing.

There is not an ultra-successful human walking this earth who hasn't embraced, and made friends with risk-taking and possible failure as *the* gateway to success.

 You are on a plateau because you are too comfortable in your status quo and you have stopped taking risks.

So, what kind of risk-taking and chance-taking are we talking about when it comes to the Go Next-Level journey? Before we move forward, I want to give you ten surprising examples of the kinds of risks I'm referring to that will launch you to your own next level. They are nothing close to the careless and catastrophic risks that most people assume:

1. Risk not being good enough.

Only by risking not being good enough, you will position yourself in opportunities for accelerated growth and expansion. If you need to be good enough, you'll stay stuck on the plateau.

2. Risk putting yourself out there and being judged

Judgment is inevitable. Especially if you're doing something big. If the fear of judgment keeps you paralyzed from essential risks, you'll stay stuck on the plateau. Your desire for more has to outweigh the fear of criticism.

3. Risk getting turned down.

We have to pursue the Go Next-Level journey with an understanding that rejection is not a reflection of your worth. Each "no" is a step toward the eventual "yes" that aligns with your path. Getting turned down can be a huge, and necessary risk.

4. Risk making a mistake.

Risk not having it all together and making mistakes. This is how we grow and learn and stretch ourselves. Errors are essential learning experiences. Mistakes are not setbacks but stepping stones toward mastery and getting off the plateau.

5. Risk losing friendships.

We'll talk more about this in Chapter Four, but to Go Next-Level, we have to risk outgrowing certain relationships. Going next-level will require you to risk questioning your social circles to see who aligns with your values and aspirations.

6. Risk taking the road less traveled.

The conventional path is the safe path, and usually the path that leaves people stuck on the plateau. An almost certain prerequisite for going to the next-level is a commitment to uncharted paths that often yields unparalleled rewards.

7. Risk not getting the job.

When you take appropriate risks, put yourself out there for possible rejection, and reach for higher places, you will get turned down. A lot. To Go Next-Level, you see rejections serve as redirections and keep moving forward.

8. Risk putting it all on the line.
Going to the next-level means going all-in. And it's scary to go all-in, so people play it safe, and get stuck on the plateau. Going to the next-level requires a wholehearted commitment to your aspirations, and nothing less.

9. Risk missing out in order to achieve something greater.
The fear of missing out is the fastest path to getting stuck on the plateau. So you take on the bad project, or you take on that bad client, and come to realize very soon it landed you stuck. Going next-level requires prioritizing your long-term goals over immediate gratifications.

10. Risk admitting that you don't know.
Take a risk with being humble. When you're humble, teachers appear to show you a better way that often fastracks you off the plateau. The admission of not knowing is the foundation for expansion.

Do these ten examples of risk-taking surprise you? These are the types of risks required to get you off the Early Peak Plateau and onto the next level.

When we say "*yes*" to these types of risks, and embrace the fears around looking weak, incapable, unfit, or whatever other adjective we can use to describe the emotion around risk-taking, it molds people into future Go Next-Level champions. When you see any and all setbacks as learning opportunities and embrace the uncomfortable feelings associated with the kinds of risk-taking above, you will launch from the Early Peak Plateau.

All of these risk-taking opportunities are a launch pad toward something greater.

Many people will be halted at the first sign of something feeling risky. Or, they'll stop when they fall down. Or they'll quit at the first setback. They'll quit because life has thrown too many obstacles their way and they just can't take any more punches. They'll pivot, try something different, and fail again. And then again. They end up *accomplishing so little* because they can't see how all of the setbacks and obstacles are *teachers* paving the way toward something greater. And so they stop too soon. They never make it to the next level because the fears around risk-taking keep them on the plateau.

People that are stuck see risk-taking as "*bad*", but to Go Next-Level, you have to see risk-taking as a necessary step.

Right now, there is an obstacle in *your* life keeping you from more and stuck on the plateau—something big and something scary and something that feels too big to accomplish, and right now the fear of this obstacle being insurmountable is holding you back from more.

But aren't you stronger than that?

Aren't you willing to lean into those necessary risks?

Aren't you willing to risk losing, and looking foolish for the sake of something better?

Aren't you willing to fail now, for the sake of what's possible in the future?

 Saying "yes" to risk-taking, and becoming friends with taking chances is the way to Go-Next-Level.

THE ULTIMATE ACT OF WEAKNESS

I haven't always thought of risk-taking like I do now. I spent the majority of my life trying to avoid risks because I experienced failure as a *shameful* event and I was too insecure to see it for the valuable asset it really was. I played it safe, found myself comfortable on my own plateaus, and gave the world the perception that I was doing great, and that I was on a great path.

That's what it looks like from the outside when you stop taking risks. It appears you have it all together. ***It's easy to look good when you don't take any chances.*** But the truth was, I didn't have it all together. I was playing life so safe because I was too insecure to take chances and risk appearing like I didn't have it all together. I didn't believe in myself; that I could handle failures, disappointment, setbacks, and looking foolish. From a place of insecurity, I thought wrongly that failure was weakness. I now know, the opposite is true.

Playing it safe and avoiding risk-taking is the ultimate act of weakness.

In my early thirties, I started working with a new coach because I realized I needed help to get where I wanted to go. I'll never forget a conversation we had shortly into working together. In fact, of all the time we spent working together, it was this one conversation I remember more than anything else. While talking about my life, my goals, and what I was trying to accomplish, he looked me directly in the eyes and said, "*I see that you are a quitter*".

Shocked by his words and stunned at the directness of his comment, it hit me like a ton of bricks. But I had no rebuttal... he was right. I was a quitter and he saw this in me. At moments when things got hard, when I really needed to stretch myself and risk failing, I found elaborate reasons to justify playing it safe. I quit relationships when they were hard. I quit new businesses when they were hard. I had a pattern of quitting just when I needed to stay the course and see something through. Because I conceptualized failing as a shameful, catastrophic event, I would quit to avoid having to admit that I failed. I didn't trust myself to be strong enough to fail, and I didn't have the confidence that if I did fail, I would be OK.

And so I never took risks that could have really propelled me to something greater. To the outside world, it might have looked like I was living a successful life, but the truth is, I was only playing it safe. *Mediocrity allows for playing it safe. Greatness requires risk taking.* I spent years stuck on my own plateau and not going to the next level because I didn't say "yes" to taking risks.

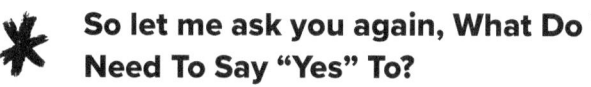

So let me ask you again, What Do You Need To Say "Yes" To?

THE ECONOMIC UPSIDE OF CALCULATED RISKS

Many people feel a resistance to risk taking because it brings up images of catastrophic scenarios where they might lose everything and end up in poverty. When you think of risk taking this way, you're imagining throwing caution to the wind, and putting everything on the line with a *careless risk*.

But that is not the kind of risk taking I am talking about. And this is not the kind of risk-taking to get you to the next-level.

I would never encourage you to take a careless risk; that would be unwise. However, to reach your optimal potential, to go to the next level, you have to take many *calculated risks*. And what I want you to see in this chapter is that calculated risks are far more easy to overcome than you realize, and they almost always involve *only risking a bruised ego*.

A client of mine named Riley is a NYC investment banker and a few years ago he was looking to make a change in jobs. Riley was doing interviews with a new potential company, and he was downloading me on the particulars of the conversation.

I asked Riley, "What is the bonus structure they're offering you?"

He said, "It's 100% of my base salary."

I said, "Why don't you ask for 200% of your base salary?"

He said, "No way....no one in the market pays that."

I said, "What is the worst case scenario if you ask?"

Riley said, "They might be so offended they won't hire me!"

Riley believed if he took a risk of asking for more money in his bonus structure, then something catastrophic would happen. He was confusing a calculated risk for a careless risk. Riley felt that asking for 200% felt so extreme, almost to the point of embarrassment, that it filled him with lots of anxiety. He said that if they say "no" to his request, he'd **"look like an idiot"**.

I reminded Riley that his catastrophic fear of them getting so offended at his asking for more money was very unlikely since the company had expressed a sincere interest in hiring him and had been pursuing him for months. I also explained that if they were so easily offended at a request for more money, then he didn't really want to work for someone like that anyway. I helped Riley see that his real problem was fearing *"looking like an idiot"*, and that fear was limiting him from reaching a possible better potential. I told Riley **he should** risk looking like an idiot.

I rhetorically asked Riley, "*Is looking like an idiot the end of the world*?" I realize that might sound insensitive when someone fears the shame of failure, but sometimes you simply have to remind yourself, ***it's only a feeling.***

Through more challenging, prodding, back-and-forth, and encouraging—and more insight from Riley about how his fears around calculated risks were holding him back—Riley mustered the courage, took a risk, and asked for a 200% bonus and they gave it to him.

In a follow-up celebratory phone call, I reminded Riley that his willingness to take a calculated risk and embrace *"looking like an idiot"* with a **simple ask** was worth $250,000. And that simply asking for more, which had very little downside outside of a bruised ego, was the most significant economic decision he'd make all year. Just a simple ask. And a risk-taking move that started moving him off his plateau.

Riley didn't ask for this bonus on a whim, with no supporting evidence he could be entitled to it. He could be reminded of his excellent performance, and strong, supporting track record throughout his career. For Riley, asking for more money wasn't an intellectual problem, it was an emotional problem. What mattered more than anything was whether Riley believed he was worth the gamble. Riley's story is a perfect example of the kinds of risks that get people off the Early Peak Plateau.

 What is the risk you need to say "yes" to that will get you moving off your plateau?

We all can relate to Riley's story. The fear of "looking like an idiot", no matter what it is, keeps us from optimizing our success and going to the next level. Because success in any area of life *requires* that we step into the fear and stretch ourselves toward more. When we do this, we may fail, but failure is never as catastrophic as we imagine it to be. And if we do fail, if we do get the "no", we will learn from it and fail forward.

In John Maxwell's book, Failing Forward, he says it this way:

"What is the root of achievement? Why do some people achieve so much? ...... When it comes right down to it, I know of only one factor that separates those who consistently shine from those who don't: The difference between average people and achieving people is their perception of, and response to failure."

THERE IS ONLY WINNING AND LEARNING

In Brazilian Jiu-jitsu (BJJ), there is a common cliche; *"In jiu-jitsu, there is no failing. There is only winning and learning."* I love this cliche and its necessary application to BJJ, because for anyone that has ever tried BJJ, you know one thing is certain; you won't always win. And if you don't conceptualize 'losing' as 'learning', the sport will be too damaging to your ego, and you'll quit. So we tell everyone in the beginning, don't worry about winning, just worry about learning. And the more you do that in BJJ, the more you'll evolve, enjoy the sport, and the better you'll get.

BJJ is a great metaphor for life, because, as in life, we get 'beat up' a lot if we're putting ourselves out there trying to do bigger and better things. Whatever it is you're trying to master in life and whatever the plateau that you're trying to launch off, however big the dream you're chasing, you can only get there with a ***mindset*** that not only embraces risk-taking and the possibility of failure, but learns to love it.

I would be a rich man if I had a nickel for everyone who walked into a BJJ class, trained for a few weeks, and I never saw them again. Someone eager to learn the sport but gets humbled by how challenging it is. They might have been a tough person in other areas of their life, or they have a long history of being a best-in-class athlete in another sport. In BJJ, it never matters. You're only one nasty submission away from being force fed a big slice of humble pie. That person, being humbled, disappears into the sunset never to be seen again. They came to 'win', they 'failed', and then they quit. The rest of their life won't go any differently.

As in BJJ, if you are trying to build a 7-figure business, create a thriving family life, start a non-profit, or apply for that big promotion at your work, you have to reframe everything about risk-taking and failure. You have to start seeing the ***truth***; going to the next level will ***require*** getting out of your comfort zone, taking a chance, and being willing to fail.

> *Failure is simply the opportunity to begin again, this time more intelligently.*
>
> **HENRY FORD**

IT'S ONLY A FEELING

It takes entrepreneurs an average of 3.7 failed businesses before they started one that was successful. Failing nearly four times before getting it right. The defeat... The letdown... The shame and disappointment... All of those difficult feelings and setbacks... All those difficult conversations explaining to friends and family why it didn't work out *yet again*...

Most people, seeing failure through a shame-based lens, would stop at failure number one and quit. They would return to the safe route instead of pushing through and seeing the failure as an opportunity to learn, grow, and push them one step closer to their most lofty goals.

Right now, there is an opportunity or a decision in your life or business that requires a risk that will take you out of your comfort zone. It's probably frightening. You know, in the deepest places of your heart, you need to go for it. It's been calling you, but you're fearful. You're afraid to go there because it feels risky and you're afraid of failing. You're afraid of looking foolish.

You're a human so you experience this fear. And the fear keeps you stuck; paralyzed and frozen in the status quo on the plateau. We all feel this way from time to time. And you might even think that because you feel this fear it's a sign you shouldn't take the chance.

But in all of my experience working with people going to the next level, the fear that keeps people on the plateau is never around catastrophic outcomes. It's **never** as-if people are gambling away their life-savings at the Roulette table and putting their families in poverty. **It's never that**. In all of my experience, what keeps people stuck more than anything else is how they will be perceived by others. It is this **root fear of shame**, and almost always this fear alone, that keeps people stuck.

Fear of other people's perception of you, and their negative judgment of you, keeps you stuck in the status quo and unable to reach those new heights beyond your wildest dreams. You fear looking stupid. You fear letting people down. You fear being perceived as a failure. And you become paralyzed with inaction when a bruised ego is at stake. It becomes crippling; keeping you from going to the next level. Becoming a Go Next-Level risk taker will require you to push through these fears.

Here are some examples of how this root-fear will manifest in our lives and keep us from launching to the next level:

» You fear looking foolish
» You fear disappointing others
» You fear disappointing yourself
» You fear looking weak
» You fear rejection by others
» You fear loss of perceived value
» You fear losing credibility
» You fear retaliation by others
» You fear loss of status
» You fear losing prestige
» You fear your own power and possibility

Despite *feeling* all of these fears, the person going to the next level pushes through. They recognize that what stands in the way between themselves and everything they want, is **only a feeling**. It's just an emotion. They know these fears exist, and they develop an appropriate "*I don't give a* _____" attitude. For the person who really wants to go to a new level, a bruised ego, looking foolish, or other people's judgements is never enough to keep them from reaching for greatness. They are willing to tolerate these feelings and take a risk anyways.

90% of the American billionaires are self-made. They don't come from money and weren't given head starts in life. How many of these people have taken chances, failed, and failed again, only to eventually make it? Do you think these billionaires are friends with failure?

Do you think they took appropriate risks where people judged them as "crazy", "foolish", or any other negative judgment? Of course this happened. These people, incredible in their bravery, despite looking foolish, became great friends with risk-taking and great friends with failure.

They knew, it was only a *feeling*.

> *Only by contending with challenges that seem to be beyond your strength to handle at the moment can you grow more surely toward the stars. Failure is a prerequisite for great success. If you want to succeed faster, double your rate of failure.*
>
> **BRIAN TRACY**

BEING UNCOMFORTABLE IS NOT A PROBLEM

Of the steps in the Go Next-Level Blueprint, embracing saying "*yes*" to risk-taking is one of the most challenging. It carries a great level of emotionality that can stunt the Go Next-Level process. Even though this can be a challenging step in the journey, remember, it's never black and white and it's never all-or-nothing. Instead, your goal is to increase your appetite for risk and move in the right direction.

In addition to getting you off the stuck plateau and launching you toward your full potential, here are some other benefits you'll experience that are worth the price of gold as your appetite for risk grows and you're willing to step into the fear:

» You are forced to grow and learn new skills
» You find out who's on your team of life, and who's not
» You recognize your self-imposed limitations
» You become more resilient by overcoming fear of any type of failure

» You tap into your dormant creativity
» You become massively more self-confident
» You become a people-magnet

The amount of upside potential for getting more comfortable with risk taking is staggering. And it's only you who suffers by not taking a chance. So let me ask you again, what do you need to say "yes" to?

GO NEXT-LEVEL ACTION STEP:

Here are a few questions to get you thinking about your own relationships with risk-taking, fears of failure, and what might be getting in the way of you reaching more. Just like in prior sections, I encourage you to actually answer these questions with pen and paper and not just read through them.

Think about your life for a minute, and find that One Thing in your life currently that feels like a risk for you. You know what I'm talking about; that One Thing that has been on your mind, keeping you up at night, the One Thing you've been avoiding, the One Thing you haven't taken the leap yet to go after it. That One risk you need to take to get you off the plateau. Think about that One Thing as you answer these questions below:

- Right now, what is that One Thing in my life I need to do that feels risky?
- What is the fear that is stopping me from doing that One Thing?
- Think about the *realistic* worst-case scenario of doing that One Thing, not the unrealistic catastrophic scenario: what is the *realistic* worst-case scenario that could happen if I take this risk?

- Who in my life do I fear the most judgment from if I take a chance on that One Thing, and it doesn't work out?
- What is the *realistic* worst-case scenario in that relationship if I felt judgment from that person?
- Imagine you are choosing to play it safe with that One Thing, as opposed to taking a risk: How is playing it safe harming me?
- What regrets might I have at the end of my life if I don't take the risk and go after that One Thing?

There is wisdom in understanding the difference in life between safe risks, and dangerous risks. What I have overwhelmingly experienced to be true in life is that we usually get stuck taking the *safe* risks. If you're reading this book, you're not a foolish person. You're not going to jump off a cliff without knowing the water is deep enough to land in. What we tend to do as humans is turn risks that are actually safe, into dangerous risks in our minds. And that keeps us stuck and paralyzed from going to the next level. To Go Next-Level, we have to *discern the difference* and be willing to take the necessary safe risks.

FAILURE IS OPPORTUNITY UNFOLDING

In order for you to get more comfortable with risk-taking, you have to have a systematic process for you to accept the possibility you might 'fail'. You also need to redefine failure in this sense too, because if you see failure for what it really is; a gateway toward greater success and opportunity to grow and learn, then failure is just the next step in the process toward greater opportunity. Let's go back to the prior section where you're thinking about that One Thing in your life that you need to take a risk on and run it through this step-by-step process for safe risk taking.

STEP #1: Inventory Your Fears & Possibilities

Oftentimes, when you think about making a change in your life, you'll tend to view it in black and white, all-or-nothing terms. In your mind, you run through all the likely scenarios of everything that could go wrong along the way, and this keeps you from just baby stepping in the right direction. To overcome this, put pen to paper and create two columns. On the left column make an exhaustive list of all your fears around the One Thing. One the right column make an exhaustive list of all the possibilities if you actualized the One Thing. When you see all of your fears versus all of your possibilities on paper, you'll immediately realize how much you're leaving on the table.

STEP #2: Accept Discomfort as Normal

You will be uncomfortable, there is no getting around it. I remember when I challenged myself to get really good at being on camera and doing more videos for my marketing. I hated being on camera and dreaded the day I would have to put the videos into the world. Shoot video. Delete videos. Shoot it again. Repeat. I was avoiding the reality that no matter how good I became on video, I would eventually have to put it out in the world and I would be uncomfortable. *Discomfort is a sign you're growing, and you need to learn to love it.* To start, I shot video only for my friends and family to watch, which made me a lot more comfortable with being uncomfortable. Accept that being uncomfortable is normal. It's only a feeling.

STEP #3: Review Your Ideal Life Daily

When you refer back to Chapter One and your Ideal Life, you know that in order to create your Ideal Life, you need to take the risks. You need to embrace failure. Referencing your Ideal Life daily, reminding yourself what you're leaving on the table, and what's at stake if you don't embrace failure, is the best motivation. My fear of doing videos was keeping me from growing my business, reaching more people, having more impact, and growing my income. I decided that feeling nervous and looking foolish were not good reasons to keep me from helping someone change their life. I reminded myself these were only feelings. I refused to let these feelings keep me from my Ideal Life.

EVERYTHING GREAT IN LIFE IS ON THE OTHER SIDE OF FAILURE

To go to the next level, it requires you to lean into risk taking, and reframe all that you believe about failure. Fears around risk taking and failure are rarely realistic catastrophic scenarios. Your fears around risk taking and failure are around the *fear of what others will think of you* if things don't go as planned. It's that simple.

We all need to learn from all of the greats that went before us. We have to see that every ultra-successful person walking the planet at some point developed a healthy "*I don't give a "_____" attitude about other people's opinions, perceptions, and the power other people can hold over us in our minds. This mindset allowed them to take the appropriate risks that catapulted them to greater places. This part of the Go Next-Level Blueprint is addressing that little voice inside your head that worries, obsesses, and gets paralyzed at the idea of losing, failing, looking foolish, or someone judging you when you make a change, take a risk, and pursue something that is right for you.

 You might fail, but so what? It's likely only a bruised ego. Risk taking is the only way to get off the plateau.

The Go Next-Level person sees risk-taking as doorways and setbacks as opportunities. Closed doors or anything else that can be perceived as a failure is actually an opportunity even if it looks and feels nothing like it. This isn't a "polly-anna-ish" spin on failure. It's looking at the reality that everything great in life is always on the other side of failure. ***We must be willing to fail*** to go to the next level.

So you, my friend, you need to take a risk. You need to take a chance. Fall in love with risk-taking because it is the gateway you have to pass through to be who you want to become.

GO NEXT-LEVEL ACTION STEP:

Earlier in this chapter, I asked you to identify that One Thing you need to take a risk on that will help you Go Next-Level. It's the One Thing that has been on your mind, that you know is keeping you stuck. Right now, before you move to Chapter Four, do one little thing that moves you one step closer to tackling that risk. One small move you can make right now. Start as small as you need to. Now, go and DO IT!

GO NEXT-LEVEL KEY-TAKEAWAYS

CHAPTER THREE: "What Do You Need to Say "Yes" to?"

→ Reaching something great requires that we **take chances**. And to Go Next-Level and get unstuck from any plateaus, it requires us to take the kinds of chances that we're scared to take.

→ Go Next-Level people do not like to fail, but they are **not afraid to fail**. The difference between going to the next level and remaining stuck on the plateau will be your perspective on risk-taking and how you perceive the possibility of failure.

→ It is only with risk-taking, and making peace with failing, that you'll ever achieve your wildest dreams and get unstuck from your plateau. People get stuck on the plateau because they stopped taking chances. And they stopped taking chances because they became afraid to fail.

→ You have to embrace the reality that taking chances often produces failures, and failures are the gateway to pass through on your way to greater levels of success. This is the irony about success and fulfillment; **success only and always follows some type of potential calculated risk**, set back, or doing something that could result in failing.

→ People that are stuck see risk-taking as "bad", but to Go Next-Level, you have to see risk-taking as a **necessary step**.

→ Right now, there is an obstacle in your life keeping you from more and stuck on the plateau—something big and something scary and something that feels too big to accomplish, and right now the fear of this obstacle being insurmountable is holding you back from more.

→ To reach your optimal potential in any area of your life, you have to take many calculated risks. And what I want you to see in this chapter is that calculated risks are far more easy to overcome than you realize, because they almost always involve only risking a **bruised ego**.

→ The fear that keeps people on the plateau is never around catastrophic outcomes. It's never as-if people are gambling away their life-savings at the Roulette table and putting their families in poverty. What keeps people stuck more than anything else is how they will be perceived by others. It is this root fear of shame, and almost always this fear alone, that keeps people stuck.

→ The Go Next-Level person **sees risk-taking as doorways and setbacks as opportunities.** It's looking at the reality that everything great in life is always on the other side of failure. We must be willing to fail to go to the next level.

CHAPTER FOUR

WHAT DO YOU NEED TO SAY "NO" TO?

GO-NEXT-LEVEL BLUEPRINT STEP #4:
RUTHLESSLY PROTECT YOUR MOST PRECIOUS ASSET

> Time is the most valuable asset you don't own. You may or may not realize it yet, but how you use or don't use your time is going to be the best indication of where your future is going to take you.
>
> **MARK CUBAN**

THE *Go Next-Level* BLUEPRINT

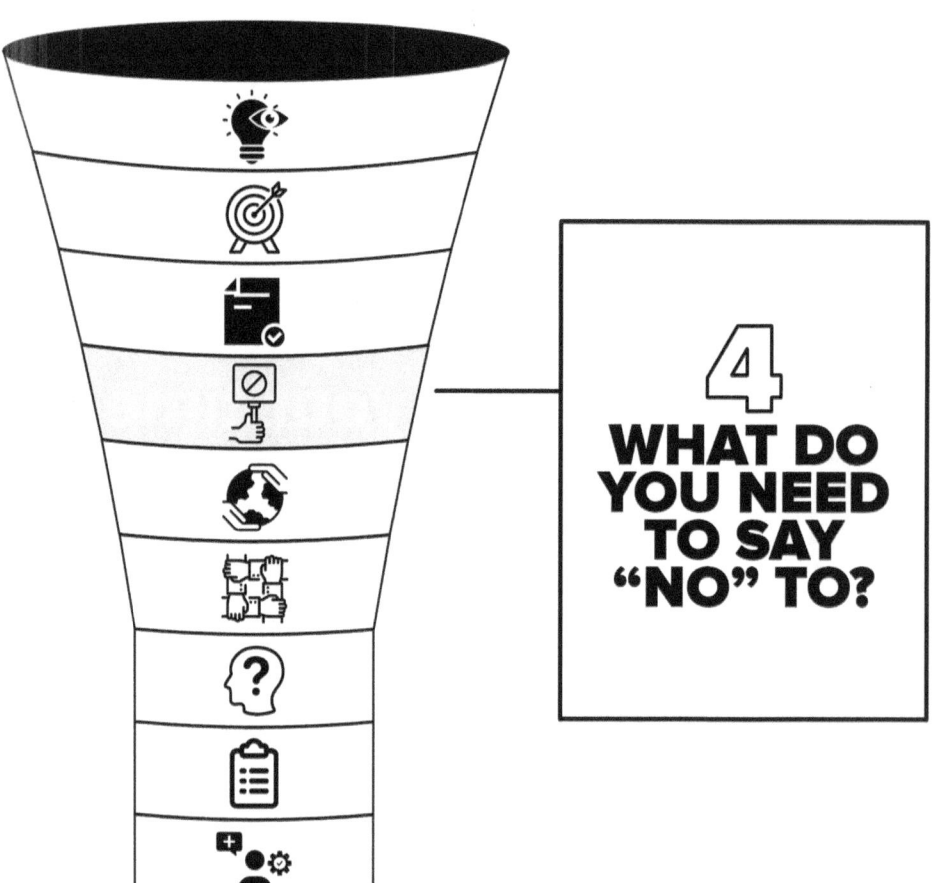

4
WHAT DO YOU NEED TO SAY "NO" TO?

RESULTS IN LIFE ARE A MIRROR WITH TIME ALLOCATION

In order to get off any plateaus, go to the next level, and fulfill everything you want in business and in life, you have to ruthlessly protect your most valuable asset; your time. It is the allocation of your time, how you spend it, who you give it to, and what you do with it that will determine the exactness of your success. Many people, who feel stuck on the plateau will never reach what they are capable of because they have never ruthlessly protected their time. They allow their time to get eaten up and occupied by people, places, and things that ultimately don't serve them in the pursuit of their Ideal Life, dreams, ambitions, and critical goals.

Many people stuck on the plateau are not intentional and deliberate about how they spend their time. They say *"yes"* when they need to say *"no"*. The weeks, months, and years click by moving them further and further away from what they really want. In the last chapter, we looked at tapping into the courage of saying *"yes"* and stepping into taking risks, and in this chapter, we're going to tap into the courage needed to say *"no"* so we can protect our time.

 Going to the next level demands we start saying "no" to things that are getting in the way of our optimal definition of success.

NOBODY ELSE CARES ABOUT YOUR SUCCESS, AMBITION, OR GOALS

There will come a point in time for every person on their pursuit to greatness when they will have to confront the conflict between time constraints, *and the life they really want to live.* In a fantasy world, we would have an abundance of time and we'd never have to make tough decisions on how to spend it. We could hang out with those friends who don't really serve us or add value to our lives, and we'd still have enough time to get everything done that mattered. We could go out every night and have drinks and dinner and laughs and celebrate wildly and still wake up early, crush our physical health goals, and have a massively productive day. We'd have enough time to binge-watch Netflix, but still continue to read feverishly to reach our personal development goals. Unfortunately, this isn't the world we live in. God created life on earth to be finite, and the clock is ticking. Time will either be your servant or your master.

 How you spend your time knowing you can't do it all, will determine the outcome of your life.

People on the Go Next-Level path are acutely aware of one salient truth: *time is the most valuable asset we have*. The person who is going to the next level has no delusions about time. They know it's moving fast and if they don't make deliberate decisions on how they're going to spend it, it'll go by in a flash and they'll wake up one day filled with regret in recognition of unfulfilled dreams.

Going to the next level requires you to protect your time with the same fervor and tenacity you would use to save a loved one in harm's way. If you knew your loved ones were in danger, you'd summon inhuman strength to make sure they were safe and well. You need to see your relationship with time this way; there are enemies everywhere; dangerous forces, dangerous people, and dangerous things all vying to take it from you; without you even knowing. These people, places and things, don't care about your Ideal Life. They don't care about your goals. They don't care about your ambition. They don't care about your success. Caring about all of those things is up to you, *and you alone*. This is a critical *mindset shift* to reach the next level.

THE SLEEPWALKING MASSES

As I write this book, my son Levi is nine years old, and my son Samuel is six. A friend recently reminded me, "You have eight more summers with Levi", alluding to the fact that once he was off to college, our special father-son relationship would never be the same. The magnitude of that reality set in for me. Having not thought about my time with my sons in those terms prior to his comment, the reality of my fleeting father-son situation and the time constraints became very real at that moment. All of the sudden, I didn't want to miss a beat with my sons. I didn't want to miss a soccer game. I didn't want to let another late night at the office go by where I didn't see them.

In *my Ideal Life*, my closest relationships with my family matter the most. In *my Ideal Life*, I have chosen to forgo certain professional endeavors for the sake of meaningful, life-giving relationships with the people that matter most to me. But that's just me, and that's *my Ideal Life*. All of us are the same, in that we all have time constraints that are either going to serve our Ideal Life, or detract from it.

 If you audited how you spent your time this past month, does your current allocation of time align with your Ideal Life?

The truth is, most people have a very casual relationship with time. Their relationship with time isn't deliberate and many people are sleepwalking through life in a hazy dream. They have no idea where they are going, why they are going there, or what they are supposed to do when they get there. That is most of the world. Most people are unconscious about the intentionality of their life, and they spend their time however the wind blows. Staring at their phones for hours scrolling the internet... Driving from appointment to appointment aimlessly... Staring at spreadsheets half-awake...

Going to the gym to workout, but not sure why exactly... Topping the night off with several glasses of wine to feel the sensation of the missing aliveness ... the feeling we get from rushes of dopamine that naturally flow when we are pursuing the exactness of our Ideal Life just as we intended to.

Our culture exacerbates this problem. *"Don't worry, you can get to it tomorrow"* they say. And there is a part of all of us that likes that idea because we never have to make any really hard decisions around time allocation. We never want to hold ourselves accountable to the reality that time is slipping away in a frightening hurry. With this laissez-faire way to look at time, we don't have to cut off relationships that drain us. We don't have to say "no" to things we shouldn't be doing. We can just keep on moving, never having to confront the tough reality that life is going by in a flash and **we only get one chance at it.**

YOU ARE THE CAPTAIN OF YOUR SHIP

I used to be a people-pleaser. I used to care so much about other people liking me and approving of me that I would pretty much say "yes" to anything. If someone asked me for a favor, I would nearly always say "yes". I convinced myself that I was being a good person, and loving, and sacrificial, by saying "yes" and that to say "no" was selfish. But the truth is it was hard for me to advocate for myself and say what I really wanted. I struggled to put my own needs ahead of anyone else's, and because of this, my time was really never my own.

I spent a lot of my life doing it this way, and because of that, I accomplished only a fraction of what I was really capable of. Lost time I will never get back...lost time that took me further off my path and more out of alignment with my Ideal Life...

 Actualizing your Ideal Life is dependent on your ability to exercise your "no" muscle.

For me personally, I lost a lot by giving my time away to people, places and things that didn't serve me. It set me back from optimizing my life. As I became more clear about my Ideal Life and **what I really wanted**, it dawned on me that so much of what I had given my time and energy to wasn't truly in service to what I wanted my life to be. And that's how life goes; if we don't protect what's ours, nobody will do it for us. This was **my job** and nobody else's.

It finally clicked with me that if I didn't ruthlessly protect my time for the purpose of pursuing my Ideal Life, the world in all of its ways would distract me and take me off course from pursuing what mattered most to me. From that moment, I made a commitment to myself that I would protect my time like a soldier would protect their comrade. I would protect myself by protecting my time. I would treat my relationship with time as a soldier guarding his post; intentionally scanning my environment looking for intruders and violators trying to cause harm. With that new commitment to myself and a new level of intensity around protecting my time, I began to accomplish goals previously far out of reach.

WHAT FORTUNE 100 LEADERSHIP CONSULTANTS DO

When we break down life in the most simplified terms, we all have twenty-four hours per day. And how you spend those twenty-four hours will determine the outcome of your life. **It's that simple.** It is the choices you will make in the finite amount of time you have. And so, if you want to live an incredible life, you have to prioritize the highest and best use of your time. You have the same twenty-four hours as everyone else, so what is going to separate you from the average? The answer is how you choose to allocate your time. To Go Next-Level, we have to change our relationship with time.

Here is how *average* people spend their time:

» On average, people spend only two hours per day on productive tasks.

» On average, people experience fifty to sixty interruptions per day, with most being nonessential.
» 82% of people don't have a time management system.
» 65% of people use their email inbox to manage their day.
» On average, people check email fifty times per day, and social media seventy-seven times per day.

The wasted time, the distractions, the internal chaos, the lack of focus. This is how average people do it, and we can see by looking at these few statistics why so much of the world will accomplish so little. It has nothing to do with intelligence, good genes, or silver spoons. It has everything to do with being disciplined with how you invest your time. Getting off the plateau and going to the next level requires you to have hard conversations with yourself around how you're spending time.

Several years ago, I had the opportunity to have a conversation with John Townsend, the multi-time NY Times Best Selling Author, Psychologist, and Leadership Consultant. John is probably best known for his book *Boundaries*, which has sold over four million copies and is used as a guide for thousands of businesses, churches, and organizations around the world. **In June**, I was given an introduction to John to schedule a Zoom meeting with him and his assistant replied back to me with his earliest available time to meet, was **in October**; five months away.

Of course, John could have moved things around to meet me sooner. He could have crammed more into his schedule to have a conversation with me sooner than five months away. But he didn't, and he modeled perfectly an example of boundaries straight out of the book he wrote. He had great boundaries, and if I wanted to talk to him, I would have to wait and be on terms *that worked for him*, not me. I appreciated and respected this role-modeling more than he could have known, and felt privileged to be on the receiving end of such great teaching. I can't speak for John, but if I were to guess,

I bet he ruthlessly protects his time. You don't achieve the kind of success John has had throughout his life and career without it.

I would bet anything that:

- » John has a time-management system
- » John spends more than two hours per day on productive tasks.
- » John doesn't get interrupted fifty times per day
- » John isn't on social media seventy-seven times per day

 Would you be courageous enough to make someone wait five days to talk to you, let alone five months?

John is an example to all of us that in order to reach our greatest potential, we have to guard our time like we've never guarded anything else. Ruthlessly guarding our time is the only way to reach our most important goals, maximize our productivity, and to perform at the highest level. And ruthlessly guarding our time requires us to see the essentialness with making people wait.

TIME KILLERS AND ENERGY DRAINERS

The Go Next-Level Blueprint requires you to evaluate your time, how you're spending it, and assess whether or not your choices around time are moving you closer or further away from getting off the plateau and moving to the next level. *There is no middle ground here*, and it requires an honest and objective look at the decisions you make every day. Consider the people you interact with, how you spend your free time, what you read on the internet, what you eat at lunch, and how you spend time with your loved ones. All of these are the simple but profound choices that illustrate your relationship with time, and how it all leads to, or detracts from getting unstuck and going to the next level.

GO NEXT-LEVEL ACTION STEP:

Grab your pen and journal and write out the answers to these questions as a way to assess your relationship with time and what you need to do differently to Go Next-Level.

- Do I have a clear system on how to prioritize tasks in pursuit of my Ideal Life?
- What tasks do I continue to do that are not the highest and best use of my time?
- Do the people I interact with each day move me **closer**, or **further** away from my Ideal Life?
- What is my most invaluable time commitment keeping me stuck?
- What distractions do I have in my daily life that are eating up precious time?
- What keeps me from finishing the most important tasks I say I want to finish?
- What do I need to cut out of my life right now that would move me closer to going to the next level?
- What activities give me increased energy, and what activities drain my energy?
- How much of my time is spent *planning* how to spend my time, versus being *reactive* to how I spend my time?
- Do the people I spend time with align with my long-term vision for my life?

When it comes to ruthlessly protecting our time on the Go Next-Level journey, we have to look at three big time-killers and plan on doing some pruning around them; our time with the *wrong people*, our time with the *wrong activities*, and our time with the *wrong distractions*. Our goal with these time-killers is to become consciously aware of how each aspect keeps us further from reaching everything we want on the Go Next-Level journey. Then, once you become more consciously aware, *you get to cut* things out that don't yield the best and right fruit.

- » **OUR TIME WITH THE WRONG PEOPLE.** Are the people you spend time with aligned with your values and your vision for your Ideal Life? Spending time with the wrong people is a guaranteed way to take you off-course from the Go Next-Level journey. It might be time for you to cut certain people out of your life.
- » **OUR TIME DOING THE WRONG ACTIVITIES.** There are certain activities that zap our energy, and if we want to go to the next level, we need *all our energy reserves* to help us get to the top of where we want to go. If you're doing activities that drain your energy, it's time to let them go.
- » **OUR TIME WITH THE WRONG DISTRACTIONS.** The world is aggressively trying to get your attention with stimulus everywhere. If you don't understand this, the world, with all its distractions will rule over your life and you won't even know it. Social media, advertisements, emails, Netflix, radio, television, YouTube, etc. These distractions rob the very limited and precious time you have, and to go to the next level they need to be cut.

 What are you willing to cut from your life right now that keeps you stuck on the plateau and further away from going to the next level?

BOUNDARIES WITH YOURSELF AND OTHERS

I was having a conversation with a friend who was apologizing profusely for not texting me back until a few hours after I initially texted him. I told him he didn't need to apologize, and that I didn't expect a response immediately and he was entitled to take as long as he needed to get back to me. I told him I wasn't going to take it as a personal slight if he didn't get back to me right away. To help my friend feel less guilty, I let him know that I only check my text messages, phone calls, and emails once per day.

I also told him that my phone was on airplane mode for most of the day, and that I was mostly not reachable—*at all*. I remember the look of shock on his face when I explained this is how I manage and protect my time from distractions. At the time, he couldn't even imagine doing something like that. So, depending on what time someone tries to get ahold of me, it could easily be twenty-four hours later until I respond to them.

But the question remains: How do we accomplish deep and meaningful work that gets us to the next level in life or business if we don't have boundaries around distractions that eat up precious time? The answer is, we don't. For me personally, I have found that people having unbridled access to me is the single biggest detriment to doing the things that matter most to me. So, I simply make myself inaccessible.

Do people in my life sometimes get frustrated by this? In the beginning, when I started making this change, they definitely did. They were used to having access to me, whenever they needed it. But over time, as I set appropriate boundaries with my time, they learned that I will respond to them eventually, but only within a time frame that works best for me. And guess what? Nobody died, and the productivity I needed to Go Next-Level skyrocketed.

Some people might say this is selfish. I say it's selfish for me not to do this. The world needs the best of me, my family needs the best of me, my clients need the best of me. The people in my life need the most energized and alive version of me, and I can only give my best when I protect my time. I share the story with you about how I've discovered what works best for how I protect my time, and now *your job is to discover what works best for you.*

> *Until you value yourself, you will not value your time.*
> *Until you value your time, you will not do anything with it.*
>
> **M. SCOTT PECK**

Here are some other examples of how people on the Go Next-Level journey ruthlessly protect their time:

- Using the morning hours when energy is the highest to work on your most important projects first, before anything else.
- Engaging in social media once per day, once per week, or completely removing social media all together.
- Creating a morning routine and an evening routine, and letting nothing get in the way of it.
- Saying "no" to meetings, social events, or relationships that don't align with your Ideal Life.
- Outsourcing every task that is not the highest and best use of your time.
- Removing television, and other distracting time-killers from your home.
- Only checking email once per day.
- Challenging yourself to completely turn off your phone for periods of time so you can do deep work.
- Making a collaborative family agreement that there will be no screen time in your home during certain hours.
- Schedule dead space in your calendar to think, contemplate, and meditate on your most ambitious dreams.

I know some of you reading this are thinking, "That seems excessive!" And the truth is, it is excessive, especially when you compare it with what most people do. But extreme levels of success require extreme measures. To launch from the plateau and go to new levels, you have to do things you weren't willing to do before, and things that most people aren't willing to do. Breaking away from average always feels extreme. Average people obsessively and compulsively look at their phones, they spend countless hours on social media, they binge drink alcohol in the evenings, and they spend time in energy-draining fruitless relationships. But you are not average.

You, on the Go Next-Level journey, are going to set boundaries around your time that some people think are crazy. **There is no other way around it.** The only people who won't think you're crazy are the people on the journey with you.

TIME IS A BANK ACCOUNT OF DEPOSITS AND WITHDRAWALS

Instead of saying "yes" to people, places, and things that don't serve you, going to the next level requires being incredibly discerning with your time. You have to protect your time like a gatekeeper; being vigilant about who and what you let through and who and what you keep out. Many people get stuck on the painful plateau because they said "yes" to things that didn't serve them. The person on the Go Next-Level journey starts saying "no" to all the people, places, and things that are keeping you on the plateau and away from your Ideal Life.

Once you start down this path, you have to say "*goodbye*" to friends that don't really serve you anymore. You have to be disciplined enough to ignore your phone when it buzzes on your desk and continue working on your important project. You have to say "*no*" to that extra drink at night because you know it's going to impact your sleep. You have to say "*yes*" to waking up an hour earlier to get started on your most important task. You have to say "*no*" to that birthday party that isn't that important. You have to say "*yes*" to spending a weekend away by yourself to get clear on your long-term vision and goals. You have to say "*no*" to that extra meeting at the office. You have to say "*yes*" to attending your daughter's recital.

Saying "*no*" is far more powerful than you realize. Here is a short list of practical benefits you'll amass when you start ruthlessly protecting your time:

» Greater *clarity* to pursue what's most important and meaningful to you.
» You *escape* the tyranny of the urgent that derails you from focusing on priorities.
» Increased physical and mental *energy* to be more efficient, productive, and accomplished.
» More white space to reflect, contemplate, and *dream* about big goals and big ideas.
» Increased sense of *control* and *autonomy* over your day, your schedule, and your life.
» Less resentment toward others when you start setting healthy *boundaries*.
» Increased *self-respect* as you prioritize yourself and your own needs.
» You become more *intune* with what matters most, filtering all unnecessary distractions.
» Greater *focus* on top priorities when you're not distracted by trivialities.
» Greater levels of *optimism* about the future.

Reaching the summit of Go Next-Level will require you to make hard decisions in service of protecting your time. But just like anything in life, learning how to set boundaries takes time, patience, and practice. Remember, *every day is a bank account*, and time is our currency. No one is rich, no one is poor, we each have twenty-four hours.

 What convenient thing do you need to say "no" to today, in order to say "yes" to that more meaningful thing tomorrow?

TOO MANY GOOD THINGS

Robert, a client of mine, is a super high-achiever. He has big goals, big dreams, and big ambitions. When I first met Robert, it was shortly after he had a devastating loss in a campaign to win a city council position in the city he lived in. It had always been a dream for Robert to get into politics, and he had spent the prior two years creating his political brand, fundraising, relationship building, hosting political events, campaigning, and even walking neighborhoods talking to residents about his political agenda and hope for change in his city.

Despite two years of focused effort, Robert failed in his bid to win city council. Running for public office was a tremendous amount of hard work, and a big part of Robert's social identity, so, naturally, the bitter sting of losing was devastating. On paper, Robert did everything right; executing a well-laid script for how to secure a city council position. But something was amiss, resulting in his loss. Robert was baffled as to what he could have done better, but after my very first conversation with him, I knew exactly why he lost.

In addition to running for city council, Robert was a serial entrepreneur. He owned two successful restaurants, ran a manufacturing company, and sat on the board for nine other organizations. And if that wasn't enough, during the campaign, he started a new non-profit to help young entrepreneurs.

When I learned all that Robert was doing, I knew instantly why he didn't win his campaign for city council. He had **too many good things** happening in his life, and the focus, mental clarity, and emotional stamina required to win public office was out of reach due to the demands of everything else in his life. I asked Robert if we could conduct a survey to gain helpful feedback on what might have gone wrong in the campaign, so he could learn about himself and what he might do differently on the next go around.

As the survey results came back, the data confirmed why he didn't win. In essence, people perceived Robert as being one-foot-in, and one-foot-out. The data suggested things like him not being "*attentive*", or "*present*" during fundraising events. People suggested in the survey data not really knowing the "*real him*", and that he seemed to often "*be in a hurry*". Instead of sticking around at events and really getting to know people, Robert spent the bare minimum amount of time before dashing off and responding to other urgent matters in his other businesses.

Robert, with too many good things going on in his life outside of his campaign, didn't give the campaign his true undivided attention it needed. He failed to build trust with his community. Robert and I both agreed that if he wanted to run again and win the next go-around, he would have to shed some things from his life in order to give more focus, energy, and attention to the campaign. I asked Robert what was more important to him, the city council position, or his involvement in the businesses and multiple non-profits? He said "*both!*". I told him bluntly, "*You can't do both, so pick one or the other*". If he really wanted to win, he would have to get good at delegating and saying "no" to other things that distracted him from the thing that was most important.

After much deliberation, Robert decided that a win for city council was his top priority, and that he would change, remove, or set boundaries around other things that distracted him from the top priority. Four years later, focused, attentive, and fully engaged with the community, Robert won the city council seat.

Robert's story is a story for many of us that have many "*good distractions*" that keep us from what's **most** important. Sometimes we must kill off the good in our lives so the great can flourish. Business opportunities, relationships, helpful activities, etc., all of which are positive and beneficial unknowingly can keep us out of alignment with the next level. For high-achievers, sometimes it can be a bitter pill to swallow when we realize we simply can't do it all, and that with our humanity comes limitations on time and energy.

 **What "good things" do you need to let go of, in order to pursue the "best things"?**

DECIDE WHAT'S IMPORTANT AND LET NOTHING STAND IN YOUR WAY

To Go Next-Level, and live a life of incredible significance, we must make some hard choices. We have to develop the wisdom and maturity to discern what should be a *"yes"* and what should be a *"no."*

We have to say *"goodbye"* to things that keep us off the path.

We have to say *"no"* to things that are not in alignment with our vision for the ideal future.

Right now, I'm saying "yes" to writing the words on this page, which means I'm saying "no" to many other really "good" things in my life. I could be enjoying time with my family, or making money working with clients, or I could be having fun with friends on the golf course. I could be playing with my kids in the backyard. I am saying "no" to many good things, in pursuit of what is most important to me in this moment. I know that if I want to achieve **my Ideal Life**, it requires me to make some daily hard decisions almost always between competing **good things**.

Reaching your version of greatness can never be achieved if you don't fully integrate this principle of ruthlessly protecting your time. The world, at large, wants your time and it doesn't care about your Ideal Life, or seeing you get off the plateau. Only you care about that, and therefore it's *all* up to you. Say *"no"* with a vengeance to anything and everything that keeps you stuck on any plateau and out of reach of going to the next level.

GO NEXT-LEVEL ACTION STEP:

Grab your pen and journal and create three columns on a piece of paper. Give the three columns the following headers: Wrong People. Wrong Activities. Wrong Distractions.

Wrong People	Wrong Activities	Wrong Distractions

For each column, decide five things you need to say "*no*" to in each category. List them on the paper and commit to yourself right now that you're saying goodbye to these things forever. It's not a debate. It's a hard goodbye. You're making a decision. Muster the discipline to stay committed to your "*no*", and stay connected to your Ideal Life vision by reviewing it often; it will be the motivation needed to make these hard choices.

GO NEXT-LEVEL KEY-TAKEAWAYS

CHAPTER FOUR: "What Do You Need to Say "No" to?"

→ In order to get off any plateaus, go to the next level, and fulfill everything you want in life and in business, you have to **ruthlessly protect your most valuable asset; your time**. It is the allocation of your time, how you spend it, who you give it to, and what you do with it that will determine the exactness of your success.

→ Going to the next level demands we start **saying "no"** to things that are getting in the way of our optimal definition of success.

→ There will come a point in time for every person on their pursuit to greatness when they will have to confront the conflict between time constraints, and the life they really want to live.

→ People on the Go Next-Level path are acutely aware of one salient truth: time is the most valuable asset we have.

→ Going to the next level requires you to protect your time with the same fervor and tenacity you would use to save a loved one in harm's way. If you knew your loved ones were in danger, you'd summon inhuman strength to make sure they were safe and well. You need to see your relationship with time this way; there are enemies everywhere; dangerous forces, dangerous people, and dangerous **things all vying to take it from you**.

→ These people, places and things, don't care about your Ideal Life. They don't care about your goals. They don't care about your ambition. They don't care about your

→ success. Caring about all of those things is up to you, and you alone. This is a **critical mindset shift** to reach the next level.

→ The truth is, most people have a very casual relationship with time. Their relationship with time isn't deliberate and many people are sleepwalking through life in a hazy dream. They have no idea where they are going, why they are going there, or what they are supposed to do when they get there.

→ Actualizing your Ideal Life is dependent on your ability to **exercise your "no" muscle.**

→ When it comes to ruthlessly protecting our time on the Go Next-Level journey, we have to look at three big time-killers:

 » Our time with the wrong **people**,
 » Our time with the wrong **activities**
 » Our time with the wrong **distractions**.

→ Remember, **every day is a bank account**, and time is our currency. No one is rich, no one is poor, we each have twenty-four hours. Instead of saying "yes" to people, places, and things that don't serve you, going to the next level requires being incredibly discerning with your time.

→ For high-achievers, sometimes it can be a bitter pill to swallow when we realize we simply can't do it all, and that with our humanity comes limitations on time and energy.

→ What "good things" do you need to let go of, in order to pursue the **"best things"**?

CHAPTER FIVE

HOW ARE YOU GOING TO SAVE THE WORLD?

GO-NEXT-LEVEL BLUEPRINT STEP #5:
IDENTIFYING YOUR MILLION-DOLLAR MISSION

> Only a life lived for others is a life worthwhile.
>
> **ALBERT EINSTEIN**

THE *GO NEXT-LEVEL* BLUEPRINT

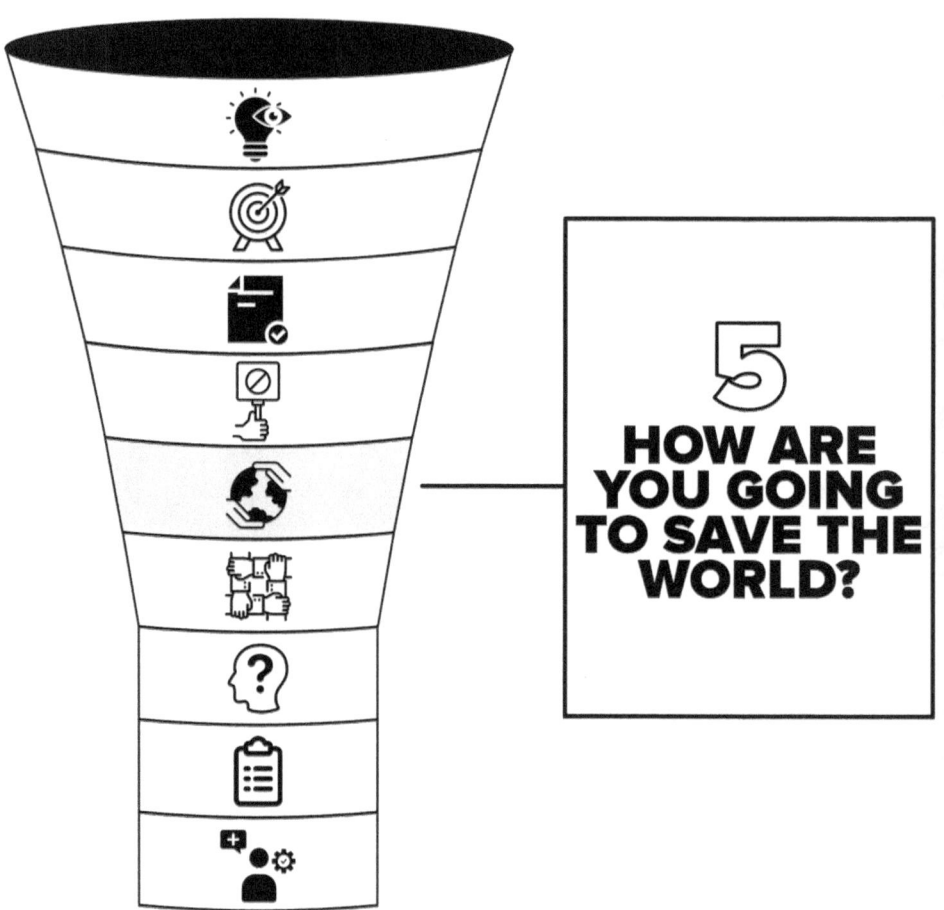

USING YOUR PASSIONS TO SAVE THE WORLD

The next stop on the Go Next-Level journey is discovering your unique problem solving capabilities, which becomes your mission. Whoever you are reading this book, wherever you've been throughout your life, and whatever your life experiences and circumstances, you have unique giftings, talents, attributes, and contributions that the world needs from you. When we understand how unique each of us are, and how we can use this uniqueness to positively save the world in our own influential ways, we become powerful mission-driven people who can accomplish anything.

When you get clarity around your unique problem solving capabilities, and you implement them toward life saving change for others, you will become filled with a sense of mission that will propel you forward even in the hardest of circumstances. One of the reasons so many people are stuck on the plateau and haven't launched to the next level is because they've been spending time in the wrong arenas of life *they're not passionate about*. And when you're not passionate about what you're doing, you'll lose steam, burnout, and become apathetic about life. Conversely, when you clearly define how your uniqueness, gifting, talents and attributes can be used to solve important missional problems in the world, nothing can get in your way.

WHAT LIFE-CHANGING PROBLEM ARE YOU SOLVING?

The most successful people and the most successful organizations in the world are unique problem solvers. We see this in every person and business we admire, from Silicon Valley start-ups changing business paradigms with new technologies, to the local painter at the art festival who produces beautiful and unique one-of-a-kind art. Success in life, and getting unstuck from any plateaus you're finding yourself stuck on, is dependent upon the acceptance of two facts:

FACT #1: You have a unique value proposition offered to the world.

FACT #2: You can use that unique value proposition to solve someone else's problem.

We cannot accelerate off the plateau and go to the next level in life or business if we are not accepting of these two facts. These two combined facts are called our ***mission***.

If we're doing something we're not passionate about, we can solve problems and become materially successful, but we will be easily miserable from a life-satisfaction standpoint because we're doing things that we're not passionate about. And conversely, if we're pursuing things we're passionate about, but not in service to others in a meaningful and world-changing way, we'll be broke, empty or unfulfilled.

So you have to do both to go to the next level; you have to accentuate your unique value proposition, and use that talent to change the lives around you. This is you on mission, and it will get you unstuck and take you to the next level.

In Chapter Two, we answered the question, *"Why Do You Want It?"* and we took a look at discovering our Big Why and understanding our purpose. In this chapter, we're going to take the emotional energy from our Big Why and discover what unique problems you can solve in the world. Whether you can articulate it or not, your life's mission resides inside you. It's time to find the answers.

> *"Outstanding people have one thing in common: an absolute sense of mission."*
>
> **ZIG ZIGLAR**

THE TENSION OF MISALIGNMENT WITH YOUR MISSION

Statistics on happiness suggest that happiness plummets around the age of thirty because it's at this age people begin believing they cannot achieve their dreams. At this age, they start to believe life is simply a utilitarian act of getting through each day without too much trouble, trying to survive to the next day. Then, a painful reality sets in that sinks happiness. Seeing life through a lens of surviving until the next day, people begin to feel nihilistic and resign all their hopes and dreams in exchange for bitterness, skepticism, and cynicism. This is people at their worst stuck on the plateau.

Sadly, this doesn't need to be the case for **anybody**. But the truth is, we haven't shown people **how to** actually discover their unique mission and pursue it to change the world. To make things worse, we are bombarded with messages from resentful people who have given up on their own aspirations that tell us to stop "*being a dreamer*", and "*buckle down*", and "*be realistic*", and to do all those things that stifle our pursuit of missional endeavors. These people tend to see life in severely black and white terms between those that selfishly pursue something deeply meaningful in their life at the cost of everyone around them, and those that deny and suppress what is meaningful inside of them in pursuit of a safer path that carries little meaning at all.

You may have forgotten what it is like to be doing something rich in meaning. You may have needed to take a safer route in life for the sake of your responsibilities. Or maybe you've taken a safer route because that's what your family or origin instilled in you? If this is true, that's understandable and good.

There's nothing wrong with taking a safe route, except when the safe route leaves us out of alignment with our life's mission, because we were all made to live on mission. If we're not connected to our mission, life won't excite us. If we're not connected to our mission, life will feel like a chore to endure. **Nobody** gets passionate about going the extra mile and tackling the world unless they're striving for their unique mission.

To Go Next-Level and fulfill everything you want in business and life, discovering your unique mission is an essential part of the matrix and it's very likely why you're on the stuck plateau. Connecting to your unique mission is the very thing that will separate you from the masses of people who are in the wrong seat on the bus. I can't do your mission and you can't do my mission. We all have missional-uniqueness that needs pursuing.

Some people attempt to get past the obstacle of pursuing their mission by making more money. There's nothing wrong with making piles of money, but if it's out of alignment with your mission there's a very good chance you will die filled with regret. Many people are sitting on top of what the world calls *'success,'* and yet still never feel like it's enough. Deep in their heart, they know something isn't right. They might wonder if there's more. But what if everything you've accomplished until now … is where the story begins, rather than how it ends? What if you've spent the last several years chasing the wrong mission? If that's a tension you feel …you are exactly where you're supposed to be; reading this chapter getting clarity on your unique mission. Until your mission is clear … no amount of money or financial gain will make you feel better or get you unstuck from the plateau you've landed on.

THERE IS NO UNIVERSAL RIGHT MISSION, ONLY A RIGHT MISSION FOR YOU

Tamara, a client of mine, is married to a very successful business owner. Throughout Tamara's marriage of 25 years, she played a very supportive role for her CEO husband. She would help organize company events, show up at company retreats, and she would always be available to play the important role of supporting cast for her husband's company. When I first met Tamara, **she was certain** she enjoyed playing this role in her husband's company, and she felt proud of the need it served. It was a good role, honorable, and her husband was openly appreciative of her impact.

Overtime, as I got to know Tamara better, she acknowledged to herself first, and confessed to me later, that she actually felt conflicted about this role she played in the company. On one hand, she knew it to be important and served the company and her husband well, and on the other hand, she didn't believe the work was her true mission.

The interesting thing about Tamara is she's an incredible artist and accomplished painter. For many years, Tamara set aside her creativity for the supportive role in her husband's business. Over the years, this caused Tamara a great deal of internal angst. No one really knew it but her, because she was skilled at presenting a rosy exterior. It wasn't Tamara's true missional-uniqueness to be a supportive cast member for her husband's business. Her true mission, her real calling in which she was supposed to save the world, was with her passion and talent for art.

For many years, Tamara dealt with low-grade depression because she wasn't fulfilling her God-given mission. Tamara was **stuck** on the plateau, because she was pursuing something that was not in alignment with her unique mission. She knew, deep within, that reveling in the joys others experienced from her art was the unique problem she was supposed to solve in the world. Helping others see the world through the lens of her art, and the life-changing perspective shifts that art can produce, was Tamara's unique problem solving capability. As an artist, she was a thriving mission-driven person. As a supporting cast member in her husband's business, she was out of alignment and just getting by.

Tamara and I agreed together that she must listen to her gut intuition and pursue her calling to fulfill her mission. Ignoring her deeper calling and not listening to her heart would mean she would experience the painful side effects of misalignment until she made a switch. Eventually, she gracefully faded out of her support role and moved more fully into her mission. Not surprisingly, the last I heard from her, she was influencing many others in a myriad of positive ways with her passions and has never looked back. Once Tamara accepted these two facts of life, she began skyrocketing off the plateau:

FACT #1: You have a unique value proposition offered to the world.
FACT #2: You can use that unique value proposition to solve someone else's problem.

AN IDEAL LIFE IS ONLY POSSIBLE BY PURSUING YOUR UNIQUE MISSION

In order to go high level and fulfill everything we want in life and business, we have to believe, and I mean really believe, that what we're doing day in and day out, is genuinely saving the world. This is not mental gymnastics. It's not just a motivational trick, or hack, it has to be felt at the deepest places inside ourselves.

You might be wondering, "*What is my mission?*". Or you might be thinking now, "*Have I been pursuing my mission?*" These are great questions I want you to continue wrestling with. Don't stop until you have both these questions pinned to the ground. And then, beat the questions while they're down. Don't stop considering your life's mission until you have crystal clear clarity. Because solidifying your mission is what gets you off the plateau and to the next level. In order for us to actualize everything we declared we wanted in our Ideal Life, whether it's financial prosperity, joy, freedom, better relationships, or fulfillment, we get it by going after our mission. Pursuing anything outside of our mission is only going to produce half measures, keep you stuck on a plateau, and will never result in maximizing what you're ultimately capable of.

Discovering your unique mission requires considering the answers to *three vital questions:*

QUESTION #1: What brings me immense joy?
QUESTION #2: What is my superpower?
QUESTION #3: What life-changing problem can I solve?

WHAT BRINGS ME IMMENSE JOY?

Discovering what brings you immense joy is an essential ingredient in cultivating your mission. If we're doing things we don't love, or doing things begrudgingly, we know we're not in alignment with our mission. We know we're in alignment with our mission when we're doing things in life that make us laugh, smile, and feel fully alive. Going to the next level isn't easy, but experiencing this next level of joy is worth the effort.

WHAT IS MY SUPERPOWER?

Your unique mission, that thing that propels you into the stratosphere of life, is always something you're good at. You have unique talents, strengths, capabilities that separate you from others, and if you're going to fulfill your mission in the world in a way that solves big problems, it needs to align with your natural gifts. When you're doing things that you're good at, you flow through life lighter and with greater ease. You're not fighting internal gravity that makes life feel hard, clunky, and forced. Identifying, owning, and operating in your strengths is essential to fulfilling your mission.

WHAT LIFE-CHANGING PROBLEM CAN I SOLVE?

Everywhere you go, when you meet someone new, imagine how your unique problem solving capabilities could impact their life. No matter who it is, you just can't help but wonder about that question. That is life on mission everywhere you go. It doesn't matter who you are, what you do, or where you come from, you have a unique ability to solve a life-changing problem in someone else's life, and in order to go to the next level, you have to see the world this way. To Go Next-Level, it requires seeing the world through a lens of the specific problems only you can solve.

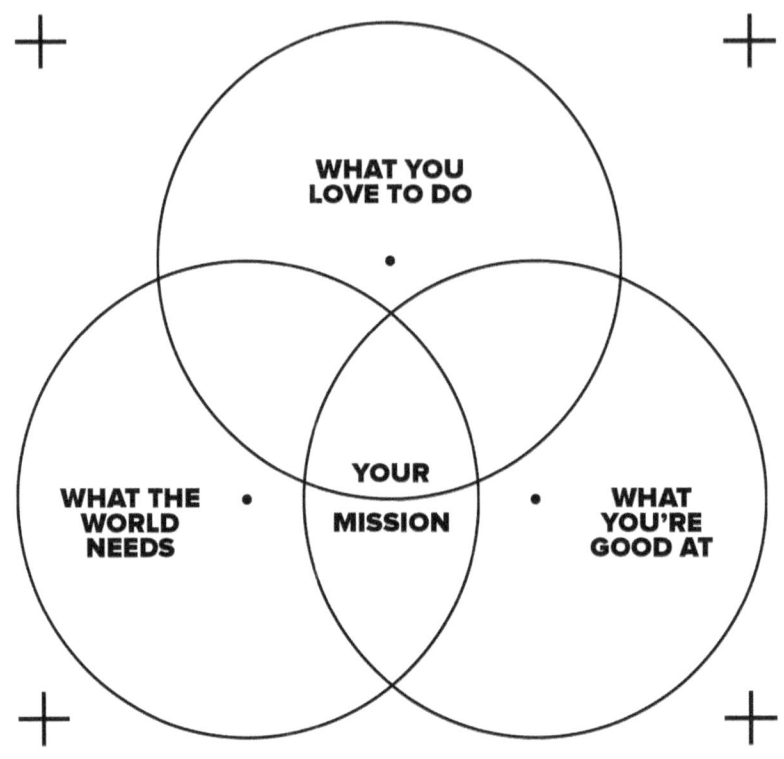

 We don't necessarily get to "choose" our unique mission, as it becomes an intersection of these 3 realities chosen for us.

YOU CAN'T HAVE SOME OF IT; YOU HAVE TO HAVE ALL OF IT

In order for you to go to the next level, you have to be in alignment with the pursuit of all three elements of your mission. If you have two working well, but not all three, you'll never reach the Go Next-Level summit.

For example, if I'm pursuing something I'm good at, and it's solving a problem, but it doesn't bring me joy, ***I'll burnout.***

Or, if I'm doing something that brings me a lot of joy, and it's solving a problem, but I'm not actually good at doing it, ***someone else will do it better.***

Or, if I'm doing something that brings me joy, and I'm also good at it, but it's not solving a problem in the world, ***no one will want it.***

GO NEXT-LEVEL ACTION STEP:

Now grab that pen and journal and go through the questions below to help you get more clarity on **your mission** and how **you** are going to save the world. As before, don't just read the questions and do this as a cognitive exercise. Write down all your answers in your journal as you'll gain much more clarity doing it this way.

- What skills, talents, or capabilities have I been praised for throughout my life?
- What am I doing that feels like fun to me, but work to everyone else?
- How can I practically make a unique dent in the universe with my contribution?
- What was the last accomplishment I completed that made me feel most proud of myself?
- What roles and responsibilities do I enjoy the most?
- What was I doing the last time I felt a deep sense of fulfillment and satisfaction?
- What talents and capabilities would the world miss if I was gone?
- If I was going to help someone breathe a deep sigh of relief, what would I be doing to make that happen?
- Why do I exist in the world?

- If I could change someone's life today, what would I be doing to change their life?
- Whose life would I most enjoy changing?
- Whose life could I most easily change with my unique talents?
- If I interviewed ten people who knew me best, what would be the common denominator in my unique way to save the world?
- What do I get complimented on by other people?
- If I got paid $1,000,000 tomorrow to solve a problem for someone, what problem would I love to solve?

These questions are designed to get you thinking about the intersection of what you're good at, what you love, and what the world needs. As you play with these questions, you'll begin to notice common themes and patterns emerge that help give you clarity on your personal mission. If you're unclear as to your personal mission, or you feel confused and foggy about it, I want you to know that's perfectly normal and nothing to be alarmed about. Getting clear about your personal mission is a big question, and it takes time, patience, and continually working through it to discover exactly what is right for you. Don't let feelings of overwhelm derail you from this process.

 You don't have to get it perfect, you just want to get it started.

THE MILLION-DOLLAR PROBLEM YOU LOVE SOLVING

You are on this earth to tap into your uniqueness and solve big problems. The quicker you can find out what that is, the sooner you're going to be on your way to reaching new levels in life and business that others just dream about. When you're pursuing your unique mission, nothing can get in your way. Fatigue can't stop you. Burnout and lack of motivation don't exist when you're on mission. Instead, you'll spend your days feeling on fire with endless drive. If life feels flat, you're likely not connected to your mission.

GO NEXT-LEVEL ACTION STEP:

Refer back to your journal and review your Ideal Life Statement. If you did your homework, you wrote some ways in how you'd love to spend your day in your Ideal Life. Pay attention to what you wrote there because there's internal wisdom connected to your mission in that writing. Your Ideal Life is the dream scenario you want for yourself in the future. It's your "**What**".

Next, refer to your journal where you wrote down notes on your Big Why. Your Big Why statement is a declaration about your life's purpose. It's identifying why all of this even matters in the first place. It's answering the question, "Why do you do what you do?". It's your "**Why**".

Now we're uncovering our mission, which is our "**How**".

Now, grab that pen and journal again and spend some time filling in the table on the next page with five items of each missional category. This will help get you started in crafting your Million-Dollar Mission. And we're not creating just any old average mission, we're creating a **MILLION-DOLLAR MISSION.** The Million-Dollar mission excites, enlivens, and feels like a powerful calling that *only you* can fulfill.

YOUR MILLION-DOLLAR MISSION

What brings you joy?	What is your superpower?	What life-changing problems can you solve?

Remember, you don't have to get it perfect right now, just fill in the table with your instinctual, knee-jerk responses. Don't overthink it or overanalyze it. For now, I just want you to write the first things that come to your mind. Eventually, we're going to take all the contents of the three categories in the table above and craft a powerful, energizing, and compelling Million-Dollar Mission Statement.

MORE OF EVERYTHING YOU WANT BECOMES A BYPRODUCT OF YOUR MILLION-DOLLAR MISSION

To live a life of massive success and significance, it takes hard work, determination, and a laser focused intensity to do what we are meant to do. When we're pursuing our Million-Dollar Mission, the hard work feels satisfying, rewarding, and so fulfilling we don't think of it as hard work anymore. We think of it as accomplishing something much bigger than ourselves. And conversely, when we're out of alignment with our Million-Dollar Mission, we'll never feel the intrinsic rewards that are only possible when we're doing what we love, doing what we're good at, and solving big problems.

Making all the money in the world but spending all your years doing it in a way that leaves you feeling empty, flat, and chronically discontent, *is not success*. You might get rich, but that's not success. However, when you pursue your Million-Dollar Mission, you will experience it all; more money, more joy, more freedom, and more fulfillment. This is the power of knowing your Million-Dollar Mission.

If you've felt stuck on the plateau, and you haven't achieved all that you know you're capable of, there's a strong possibility it's because you've been operating outside of your mission. If you want to achieve more financial freedom, more prosperity, more time freedom, more joy in your work and at home, and feel a deep sense of contentment at the end of a long day, you **have to operate inside your mission**. When you're operating outside your mission, life feels unsatisfying and leaves us in a hurry looking for meaningless retirement. Here are a few very tangible benefits for people who are living on mission:

» **YOU WILL BE CONSTANTLY MOTIVATED:** Motivation comes easy when you're doing what you *love*, what you're good at, and you're saving the world. People that lack motivation are always living outside their mission.

- **YOU WILL RARELY FEEL BORED:** When you start to realize what's at stake for you living outside your mission, you'll rarely feel bored. Living your mission is energizing, stimulating, and massively *enlivening*, and it's impossible to feel bored when you're creating meaningful change in the world.
- **YOU WILL FIND IT EASIER TO MAKE DECISIONS:** When people struggle with making life decisions, it's almost always a byproduct of being unclear about their mission. When we know our mission and we're living it out, we don't have to make as many decisions because they've already been made for us. Living on mission makes us certain about our actions, and gives us a tremendous amount of *focus*.
- **YOU WILL ACCOMPLISH MORE:** Living out your mission is the *turbo-boost* for you to accomplish things you never thought possible for yourself. Every great accomplishment for mankind has been a result of someone living out their mission. When you have a clear mission, get ready to be a producer.
- **YOU WILL DEVELOP A SENSE OF BELONGING:** When you're living on mission, you start to ***attract*** other like-minded people who can relate and resonate with your mission. If you feel isolated, alone, and like you're living on an island, but you're surrounded by people, there's a good chance you're living out of alignment with your mission.
- **YOU WILL HAVE NO REGRETS:** People with regrets are always people who didn't listen to that little inner voice calling them into their mission. They knew they were supposed to do something *significant* with their time, but they turned away from it. In the end of your life, you will never say you regretted pursuing your mission.
- **YOU WILL MAKE MORE MONEY:** If you look at the wealthiest people in the world, they have a clearly defined mission and their wealth is a byproduct of that mission. Money becomes a result, or a consequence of people honing in on what they love,

what they're good at, and using that to solve big problems in the world. When you're on fire for your mission, it's no surprise that wealth follows.

 When we realize all of the benefits from integrating our mission into our lives, you won't want to spend another day pursuing life without it. What are you waiting for?

PURSUING YOUR MISSION IS THE ONLY WAY TO HAVE IT ALL

As I write this page, it's fall of 2023 and we're on the backside of one of the most significant labor market events in history; the Great Reset. As a result of many factors such as COVID-19, the lockdowns, working from home, federal economic stimulation, and many other considerations, corporations are desperate to find skilled labor because people have left the labor market in droves. Without getting into the political aspect of this point, what I want to pay close attention to is the fact that many people making *great money* and working *great jobs* decided to quit. **They walked away from it all.** They left the security and stability of a good paycheck to go pursue what was more meaningful to them.

As disruptive as the global pandemic has been, it also became a great invitation for many people to reflect, analyze, and reconsider how they want to spend the rest of their days. Many people left soul-draining *"good"* jobs which were out of alignment with their mission, to take a chance on themselves in pursuit of their mission. They might not have known it this way, or said it this way, but that's exactly what happened for millions of people.

Adrian, a client of mine, owned several restaurants in California that were forced to shut down at the beginning of the pandemic in the Spring of 2020. Adrian sat idly by as his restaurants closed down. All the hard work, blood, sweat, and tears were washed down the drain. He was left wondering what he was going to do in the aftermath of his businesses collapsing. At first, Adrian was understandably panicked, anxious, and angry at the loss of his restaurants. But then something remarkable happened. Adrian went on an inward journey of self-discovery to understand what he really wanted and was most important to him. He was forced to consider his mission. Adrian had two of the three parts right: Adrian was a successful restaurateur, and his businesses solved a problem; they provided people a great experience to enjoy good food, good drinks, and human connection. But what Adrian didn't realize while he owned his restaurants, that he was only able to realize in the aftermath of his restaurants shutting down, was that *he didn't love owning restaurants.* He was missing the third ingredient in the Million-Dollar Mission.

He was good at it, but he didn't love it, and therefore he was out of alignment. This misalignment had taken a toll on him. In hindsight, Adrian reflected and saw how much life-chaos the restaurant business had actually caused him. The late nights, the hours over the weekend, the cashflow roller coaster, etc. Two divorces... Struggling with health issues... Financial instability... Overwhelming amounts of stress... Owning restaurants had actually been killing Adrian. Years being stuck on the plateau, all along he had thought he was pursuing his calling. For some, owning restaurants is their mission, it just wasn't Adrians.

The Great Reset turned out to be the biggest gift for Adrian because it forced him to stop doing what he didn't love, and he probably wouldn't have come to that conclusion on his own. Once the shock of losing his restaurants dissipated, Adrian not only accepted his fate, but celebrated the gift of clarity he had been given. Adrian could never have reached the Go Next-Level pinnacle owning restaurants. Although his restaurants were financially successful, they came at a great cost to his emotional, physical, relational, and spiritual health. And in the end, the financial gain was never worth the loss he felt to other critical aspects of his life that mattered more.

Currently, Adrian is using his knowledge of the restaurant business, his love for creating environments for people to connect and gather, and his wide network of relationships, to create private equity funds to raise start-up capital for new restaurants. Adrian is out of the day-to-day operations of owning his own restaurant, has better balance in his life, is making more money than when he owned the restaurants himself, and is immensely more fulfilled on this side of the business. Adrian is on mission now, and wakes up every day excited to tackle the world, something he rarely felt before.

The global pandemic was an opportunity for many to take stock, and reevaluate their lives, and consider whether or not they were living on mission. Most people who made a big change during the Great Reset would have said something like, "*I'm just not happy*", or "*I just can't do that job anymore*". All of these people were describing the internal conflict and inner struggle that exists when we're not pursuing our mission.

This is the power of needing to fulfill our mission.

So let me ask you:

Are you pursuing what brings you immense joy?

Are you using your superpowers?

Are you intentionally solving a life-changing problem for others?

There is only *one* of you. That's it. And it's your job, with the help of others that know you, to answer these critical questions. If you can't answer a definite "*Yes!*" to all three of these questions, it's time to start making changes. The pain of living misaligned with your mission only gets worse with time, never better.

To get to the next level, pursuing your mission *is the only way*. Sure, you can make good money doing things outside of your mission, but you'll never be truly satisfied and deeply fulfilled. There are millions of those people. Massively rich and massively miserable. You can get by doing things outside of your mission, but you'll never feel that deep, powerful sense of contentment and fulfillment that is only possible when you pursue your mission with every fiber of your being.

GO NEXT-LEVEL ACTION STEP:

By pursuing your mission, you'll be able to actualize Go Next-Level and getting unstuck from any and all plateaus. This is how you get to have it all. Now, I want you to craft five versions of your own Million-Dollar Mission statement before you move onto Chapter Six in the Blueprint, and remember, you don't have to get it perfect, you just have to get started. Remember, your mission is a living, breathing, organism that evolves with time, so let's just get something on paper today, and we can always go back and refine and adjust as needed later on.

Here are a few examples of other Million-Dollar Mission Statements to help you get thinking:

- Igniting transformation through my passion for animals and children, I am committed to creating a therapeutic horse ranch that empowers Autistic children not just to survive but to truly thrive.
- Empowering young women is my mission. Through the indispensable skills of financial management, I pave the

way for a future of young women defined by prosperity, stability, and unwavering self-reliance.
- I am the force behind global leadership development, spearheading transformative leadership programs that propel millions of leaders to unprecedented heights of leadership success.
- Pioneering the future of digital success is my mission. I am committed to revolutionizing digital marketing expertise for all to access.
- Standing as the unrivaled CPA authority in my region, I champion mid-sized businesses to overcome unraveling complex tax challenges with precision, saving time, money and overwhelming stress.
- Elevating the standard of home-building is my commitment. I instill unparalleled peace of mind with each home I build that stands as a testament to enduring quality, safety and lasting legacies.

Use these above examples for inspiration in creating five versions of your Million-Dollar Mission Statement that feels exciting, challenging, and something that will get you jumping out of bed to pursue. People who have gone to the next level of life and business are all chasing their mission, and discovering *your* mission will be the biggest gift you can give yourself and the world. This is your calling to join me and all the other people who've launched to entirely new levels in life and business by discovering their unique life-changing mission and never looked back.

GO NEXT-LEVEL KEY-TAKEAWAYS

CHAPTER FIVE: "How Are You Going to Save the World?"

→ When we understand how unique each of us are, and how we can use this uniqueness to positively save the world in our own influential ways, we become powerful **mission-driven people** who can accomplish anything.

→ One of the reasons so many people are stuck on the plateau and haven't launched to the next level is because they've been spending time in the wrong arenas of life they're not passionate about. And when you're not passionate about what you're doing, you'll lose steam, burnout, and become apathetic about life.

→ Conversely, when you clearly define how your uniqueness, gifting, talents and attributes can be used to solve important missional problems in the world, **nothing can get in your way.**

→ Success in life, and getting unstuck from any plateaus you're finding yourself stuck on, is dependent upon the **acceptance of two facts:**
  » **FACT #1:** You have a unique value proposition offered to the world.
  » **FACT #2:** You can use that unique value proposition to solve someone else's problem.

→ We cannot accelerate off the plateau and go to the next level in life or business if we are not accepting of these two facts. These two combined facts are **called our mission.**

→ If we're doing something we're not passionate about, we can solve problems and become materially successful, but we will be easily miserable from a life-satisfaction standpoint because we're doing things that we're not passionate about. And conversely, if we're pursuing things we're passionate about, but not in service to others in a meaningful and world-changing way, we'll be broke, empty or unfulfilled.

→ So you have to do both to go to the next level; you have to accentuate **your unique value proposition,** and use that talent to change the lives around you. This is you on mission, and it will get you unstuck and take you to the next level.

→ Some people attempt to get past the obstacle of pursuing their mission by making more money. There's nothing wrong with making piles of money, but if it's out of alignment with your mission there's a very good chance you will die filled with regret.

→ Many people are sitting on top of what the world calls 'success,' and yet still never feel like it's enough. Deep in their heart, they know something isn't right. They might wonder if there's more. Until your mission is clear ... **no amount of money or financial gain** will make you feel better or get you unstuck from the plateau you've landed on.

→ In order to go high level and fulfill everything we want in life and business, we have to believe, and I mean really believe, that what we're doing day in and day out, is genuinely saving the world. This is not mental gymnastics. It's not just a motivational trick, or hack, it has to be felt at the deepest places inside ourselves.

➤ Discovering your unique mission requires considering the answers to **three vital questions:**
  » **QUESTION #1:** What brings me immense **joy**?
  » **QUESTION #2:** What is my **superpower**?
  » **QUESTION #3:** What life-changing **problem can I solve?**

➤ We don't necessarily get to "choose" our unique mission, as it becomes an **intersection of these 3 realities** chosen for us.

➤ Your Ideal Life is the dream scenario you want for yourself in the future. It's your "What". Your Big Why statement is a declaration about your life's purpose. It's your "Why". Now we're uncovering our mission, which is our "How".

➤ If you've felt stuck on the plateau, and you haven't achieved all that you know you're capable of, there's a strong possibility it's because you've been operating outside of your mission. If you want to achieve more financial freedom, more prosperity, more time freedom, more joy in your work and at home, and feel a deep sense of contentment at the end of a long day, you have to operate **inside your mission.**

CHAPTER SIX

WHO IS GOING WITH YOU?

GO NEXT-LEVEL BLUEPRINT STEP #6:
BUILDING YOUR UNSTOPPABLE LIFE-TEAM

> Deliberately seek the company of people who influence you to think and act on building the life you desire.
>
> NAPOLEON HILL

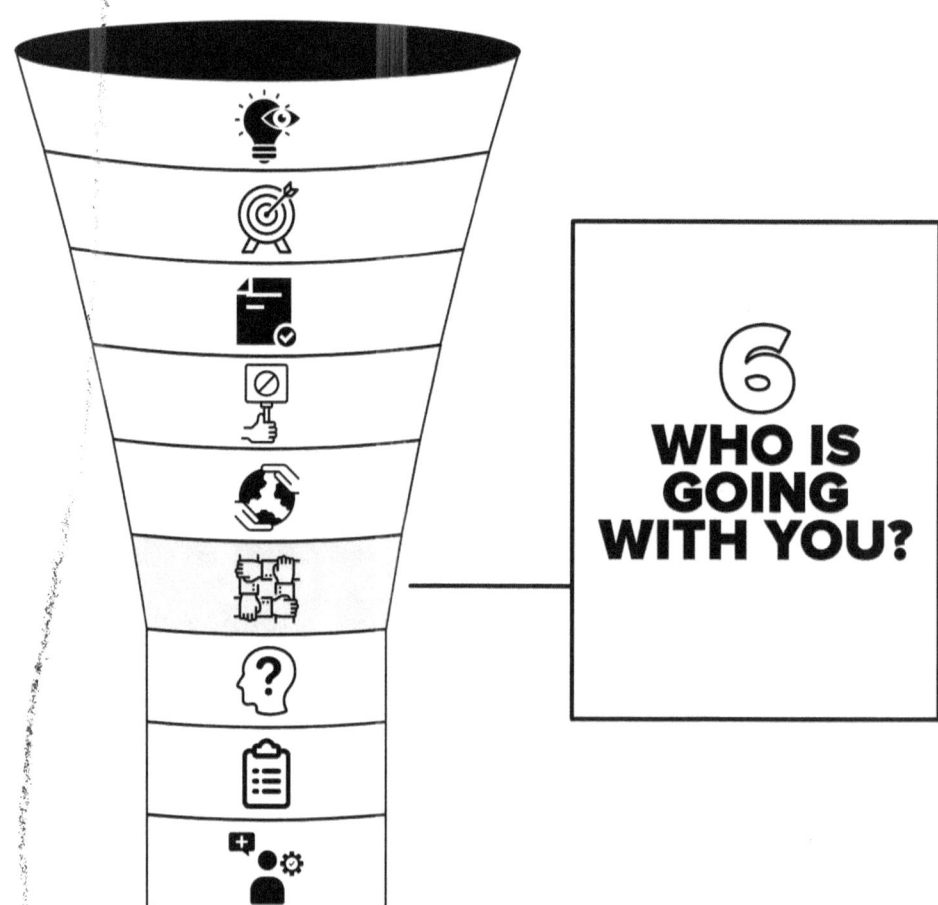

YOU MIGHT BE GOOD, BUT YOU NEED OTHERS TO BE GREAT

We can't go to the next level alone. No matter how good we are, we need others to be great. If we want to Go Next-Level, and launch from any plateaus, we have to have a team of people in our lives that will challenge us, encourage us, support us, grow us, stretch us, and hold us accountable to move in the direction that matters to us. It is easy and certainly possible to have *some level of success* on your own and without the intentional surrounding of key other people, but it is not possible to go to the next level without them.

On your own, you're confined by the limitations of *your* thinking, *your* imagining, *your* creativity, and *your* beliefs of what is possible for you. It's only when you surround yourself with right other people who can see what you cannot see that you'll make it past stuck plateaus and fulfill what you want in life and business. This group of people we intentionally surround ourselves with is called our Life-Team.

Our Life-Team is our personal Board of Directors we intentionally and deliberately appoint to be the council we go to for help with tough life decisions and support when we need it. Our Life-Team also comes to us when we need to be challenged or when we need course correction. Our Life-Team understands our vision for the ideal and acts as our guardrails to make sure we're staying on the path we've declared important to us.

A Life-Team consists of a mix of three key relationships:

1. **MENTOR:** A Mentor is someone in your specific industry who helps you grow with specific knowledge, expertise, and wisdom. The Mentor helps you with *Strategy*.
2. **COACH:** A Coach is someone who is intentionally outside of your specific industry that helps you reach ambitious goals by being a thought partner, a problem solver, and giving you objectivity. A Coach helps you see what you cannot see, and helps you with *Clarity*.

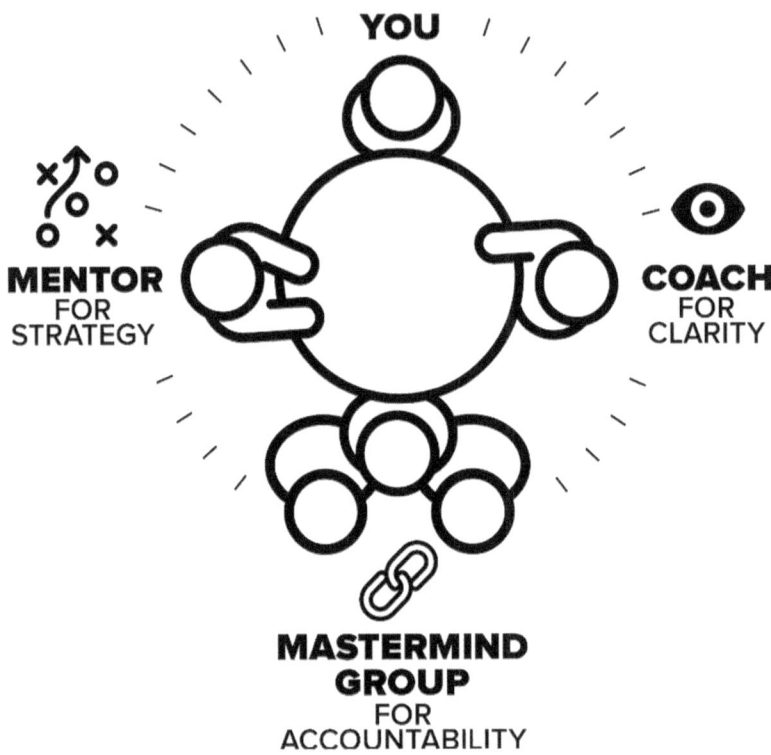

3. **MASTERMIND GROUP:** A Mastermind Group is a peer group of like-minded individuals who share your value system related to growth, expansion, and achieving optimal success. The mastermind group helps you with ***Accountability***.

No matter what we are trying to architect in our Ideal Life from Chapter One, we need all three of these relationships to make it happen. If we lack any one of these key people, we will remain stuck on the plateau. The truth is the majority of people who feel stuck and plateaued are often living on their own private island of isolation and disconnection. They live here for two main reasons:

1. **LACK OF AWARENESS:** They haven't understood the immense value of what having a Life-Team can do for them.
2. **LACK OF TRUST:** They have a hard time trusting other people and don't feel comfortable having others speak into their lives.

So, because of these main two reasons, most people set out in life and business on their own with a chip on their shoulder, doing things on their own, their own way, and without the relational components necessary to Go Next-Level. In many ways, this sense of doing it your own way, and on your own, can be a powerful attribute that creates resiliency, self-reliance, and personal determination. These are great qualities, and we don't want to lose those. But those qualities will only take us so far, to a point where we find ourselves on the Early Peak Plateau. At some point, we need to combine those qualities with the necessary wisdom of the right others to go to extraordinary levels.

The character attributes of resiliency, self-reliance, and determination eventually become character deficits that keep people stuck and unable to move to the next level. Without the intentional surrounding of the right others to help grow you, challenge you, stretch you, and help you think new thoughts, you will only grow to the level of your own capacity. You can reach *good on your own*, but you'll never reach *great on your own*.

No matter how bad you might want it, you can't get around the reality that, as a human, you are limited and insufficient on your own, and your optimal success relies on who you're surrounded with.

THE FISH WILL GROW TO THE SIZE OF THE TANK

"How big will the fish get?" I asked the salesman at the pet shop while shopping for a pet fish with my son. "In the wild, this particular fish would be about five times as large as it is now, but the fish will only grow as big as they can fit in their habitat". This fish, which had a great capacity for being much larger, would *adapt* to the small fish tank and *literally stop growing* because its habitat was too small. And this is what happens to people who are stuck and plateaued. *They have put themselves in an undersized tank by surrounding themselves with undersized people.* They live in small habitats, not even knowing there is a whole expansive ocean waiting for them to explore.

 Going Next-Level requires getting into the bigger tank of bigger people.

Because to Go Next-Level isn't easy, we need the right people in our corner that can guide us there. We need the right people to stretch us into reaching our Ideal Life. We need the right people to remind us of our Million-Dollar Mission when we get off course.

Without the right people, we're going to be confused, unsure, and doubtful. Taking all sorts of wrong turns. Without the right people, we'll take painful shortcuts and cheat ourselves. Without the right people, we're guaranteed to make costly errors that will make the journey to the Ideal Life costly and a painfully unnecessary winding road that never sees a finish line. Small results happen alone, next level results happen only with a team of the right others.

> "If I have seen further, it is by standing on the shoulders of giants."
>
> **ISAAC NEWTON**

When I think about the Life-Team principle even for my own life, I see a very clear line of demarcation when I broke free from the trap of being a lone soldier to having the right people in my life to grow me, stretch me, challenge me, and support me. Prior to this change, I was ultra-independent and I prided myself on doing everything on my own and without help. I thought that it was a badge of honor to succeed on my own. But when I found myself stuck living on my own painful plateau, I knew I needed the collective wisdom of the right others to get unstuck. Without the right others, I was confined by my own limited ideas, limited thinking, limited creativity, and limited paradigms. I was in a little fish tank unknowing there was a huge expansive ocean available to me.

So, I humbled myself, admitted defeat in realizing I couldn't get where I wanted to go on my own, and brainstormed a list of Life-Team members, and made it a priority to seek advice from people much smarter, and much further along than me. Since the inclusion of my Life-Team, my life and business have never been the same. Everything good in my life; my health, my family, my company, is because it's been challenged and grown to a new dimension by the right other people. Something I could never have done on my own.

If you're reading this and you've prided yourself on getting pretty far on your own, give yourself a pat on the back. You've kicked butt. Truly. But now it's time for a change. The old way doesn't work anymore. The old way will keep you on the plateau. Don't let your personal feelings of pride for the success you've built on your own become your Achilles heel and keep you from going to the next level. Going Next-Level is now a team affair.

THE MYTH OF THE MARLBORO MAN

I grew up in an era where cool people smoked cigarettes. All the actors, professional athletes, and famous people were all seen smoking cigarettes, and the iconic Marlboro man who starred as the brand for the cigarette company was no different. He was a badass; on his horse in the snowy Wyoming country, all by himself, herding cattle, fighting off nature's predators, and sleeping alone under the stars. He was the icon of rugged individualism and admired by so many little boys. Every little boy growing up in the 1980's had a part of him that wanted to be like the Marlboro man; deeply self-sufficient, ruggedly individualistic, and pridefully resilient.

All of these qualities are admirable. But these attributes, like all attributes, can become deficits if not properly balanced. These attributes are never **all good**, or **all bad**, we just need to know when to use them and when to shut them off. For nearly every single person who's stuck on a plateau, the individualistic and self-sufficient attributes that were helpful in reaching a certain level of success, become the same attributes that stunt reaching greater heights of success. As the cliche goes, *"The things that got you here, won't get you there."*

The Life-Team concept challenges the individualistic and self-sufficient mindset. Creating a Life-Team acknowledges you need help from the right people to reach your fullest potential, because **you are always going to be limited** by your best thinking, your best ideas, and your best lens in which to make decisions. Your best might be good, but the best of a multitude of smarter and wiser people is needed to get you to great. Step #6 in the Go Next-Level Blueprint sidelines self-sufficiency and replaces it with a personal Board of Directors.

Having a Life-Team will take you to the next level in multiple ways:

» You will move from being isolated where you say, "*I don't need anybody*", to key relationships with the right people where you say, "*I can't do it on my own*".
» You will move from individualistic thinking that says, "*I have the answers*", to collective thinking, where you say, "*Let's put our heads together and find the answers.*"

» You will move from pride, ego, and insecurity keeping you from asking for help from the right people, to humility, where you gladly raise your hand and ask for support that will elevate you.
» You will move from a scarcity-mindset where no one can be trusted, to a growth-mindset where you rely on a handpicked community for guidance.

To get off the plateau and Go Next-Level, we need to understand and see the immense value of having many select others in your life. And when we experience how powerful the select collective can be over the individual, you'll never turn back to doing things on your own again. This section of the Go-Next-Level Blueprint illuminates the reality that eventually you will plateau because you'll only go as far as your own thinking and capabilities. That's when you need to create a systematic Life-Team of the right other people to challenge you, grow you, stretch you, and support you to go to a whole new level that is simply impossible on your own.

Many of us have lived with an admiration of people like the Marlboro Man and the rugged individualism he embodies. We've prided ourselves on cliches like being "self-made" and the positive feelings we get from that idea. And if you continue to chase that feeling of self-sufficiency, you will stay stuck, and your potential will be severely limited. The truth about the Marlboro Man; if he were a person in real life, he would struggle because he's living incongruently with the natural design for optimal human functioning. To Go Next-Level, you need to put a cog in the wheel of any "self-made" limiting thinking, isolation, and being disconnected from people who can take you further.

**If you want to go fast, go alone.
If you want to go far, go together.**

MAKE FRIENDS WITH HUMILITY TO ACCELERATE YOUR GROWTH

To Go Next-Level and reach more than you ever thought possible, humility is a cornerstone character requirement. It's only in humility where we can acknowledge that we don't know what we don't know. And in this place of humility, realizing we don't know what we don't know, we reach for help, guidance, and assistance from the right others to take us to levels not possible to reach on our own. With humility, we ask questions, we get feedback, we get challenged, we find support, and we discover new layers of truth.

We can't do any of these things without humility.

It's not uncommon for people to reach a certain level of success on their own, **but never the kind of success that makes you unstoppable.** Not the Go Next-Level kind of success. The gate to Go Next-Level success is locked unless you bring the right people with you. It's that simple. It's only in the surrounding yourself with key people that you'll reach heights never thought imaginable for yourself. We don't need to look far to see a world filled with marginally successful, burnt-out, and unhappy people who all share a common quality: Isolation. A combination of a lack of awareness and too much unhealthy pride keeps them from taking higher level people on the journey with them that would exponentially accelerate their achievements. *Some people would rather fail, than ask for help.*

And the truth is, no one likes having another person speak into their life; challenging them, questioning them, and holding them accountable. There isn't a person alive who says, "I love that, give me more of that!" But the people who are going to the next level "take their licks" and see the necessity of this feedback system to rise to extraordinary levels. **Weak people do it alone. Strong people ask for help.** Without the power of a Life-Team, you will never reach your potential.

THE #1 REASON PEOPLE FAIL

When we look around at the people who have reached incredible heights in life, both personally and professionally, we'll see an entourage of relational support systems around all of them, in every domain of their life. They know that in order to reach great heights in any domain of their life, they need to seek the wisdom of others who know more than them.

 Great people intentionally seek the company of other great people.

For example, the former CEO of Google, Eric Schmidt, said the best advice he ever got was to hire a coach. In an interview with Fortune Magazine, he said he resisted at first, but eventually changed his mind and went on to say that "everyone needs a coach". Bill Gates, who worked with a coach for all of his career as CEO of Microsoft, said in a 2013 TED talk, "Everyone needs a coach. It doesn't matter whether you're a basketball player, a tennis player, a gymnast, or a bridge player. We all need people who will give us feedback. That's how we improve."

No one gets to the top by themselves. You need to be surrounded by people who want to see you succeed, people better than you, and people that will do what it takes to make sure you get there. This is the role of your Life-Team.

After coaching elite-performers for nearly two decades, I've seen an incredible amount of high-level successes, and I have seen many catastrophic failures. I've had the privilege to learn from both ends of the spectrum, and in all my experience, I can tell you the single biggest factor that results in failure: ***Doubling down on a bad decision.***

Whether it's doubling down on a bad decision that will destroy your family, or one that will destroy your business, it's always the same. I've had many sleepless nights being witness to businesses, families, and careers falling to pieces because someone double-downed on a bad decision that could have been prevented with the right people in their corner. A Life-Team helps you steer the ship away from impending doom.

In life, we are going to make bad decisions and we are going to make mistakes. That's just the way it goes. But without a Life-Team, we often double down on those bad decisions and those mistakes. We don't have clarity and we can't see the big picture, and often our decision making is emotional and not trustworthy. We're locked into our own paradigms of bad thinking. So instead of making one bad decision and course-correcting, we make two, and three and four bad decisions, until it becomes a crisis that results in catastrophic failure.

I've been part of people's Life-Teams, and people have been part of my Life-Team and together, as a collective group of people that are all rowing in the same direction toward greatness and mutually understood goals and values, we have averted crises together time and again. What I couldn't see, someone else was able to see. What someone else wasn't able to see, I was able to see for them. This is the power of not going it alone.

As you get closer and closer to the top, ***the stakes for bad decisions get higher and higher***, and the need to have a team of people who help in decision making becomes much greater. With a powerful Life-Team in your corner, you're eliminating the potentially devastating tendency to double-down on a bad decision. You have multiple sets of eyes, and ears, and perspectives, and a collective wisdom you can rely on to point you in the right direction.

 You cannot put a price tag on the value of something like this.

In order to Go Next-Level, you have to surround yourself with the right kinds of people that can help you reach the top. ***You can make it to the plateau without a Life-Team, but you can't get off the plateau without one.*** Grab your pen and journal, and rate yourself on a scale of 1-10 on the questions below to assess what kind of Life-Team you're currently using and whether or not you need something more in this area.

- Do I have key people in my life who intimately know my goals, dreams, and long-term plans? (Answer on a scale of 1-10)
- Do I have people in my life who intimately know my daily schedule, daily routines, and short-term objectives? (Answer on a scale of 1-10)
- Do I have people in my life in which I heed advice, feedback, correction, and challenge regarding **professional** or business decisions? (Answer on a scale of 1-10)
- Do I have people in my life in which I heed advice, feedback, correction, and challenge regarding **personal** life decisions? (Answer on a scale of 1-10)
- Am I comfortable making big decisions independently and without the input from others? (Answer on a scale of 1-10)
- If everything was falling apart in my life, do I have someone I feel comfortable and confident calling at 2:00 a.m. to walk me through it? (Answer on a scale of 1-10)
- Can I name the handful of people I collaborate with regularly when making key life decisions? (Answer on a scale of 1-10)
- Are there people in my life, outside of my spouse, CPA, or my financial planner, who know the intimate details of my financial situation? (Answer on a scale of 1-10)

Where do you find yourself stacking up on that 1-10 rating? Which question did you score the lowest? Highest? The purpose in working through these questions is to illuminate certain areas of your life where you ***need the right people*** in your corner to help take you to the next level. Maybe you have some, but not all. Or maybe you thought you had them all, but you realized you need to make some changes to your roster. Wherever you're at in your own Life-Team cultivation, use today as an opportunity to evaluate, assess, and reflect on this necessary ingredient in the Go Next-Level journey.

 Remember, you can't get off the plateau by yourself.

ASKING FOR HELP IS THE HARDEST RISK WE EVER TAKE

One day, Joel, a good friend of mine, called me and told me he got promoted to CEO of his company. I knew Joel had been wanting that position for some time so when he told me the news, I was thrilled for him. As quickly as I could congratulate him, the conversation quickly turned to him letting me know how hard of a time he was having. Joel explained to me that as soon as he stepped into the CEO role, he learned quickly just how dysfunctional the company actually was. Now it was his job to turn things around and he felt completely overwhelmed. Joel was out of his league and feeling tons of pressure to perform, and knew he needed help to be successful in his new role as CEO.

Joel shared with me that he wasn't sleeping at night, and the stress of this job had totally overtaken him. I knew Joel was more than capable of handling this position because he was incredibly bright, hardworking, and a tremendous leader with high-level people skills. So, I encouraged Joel to not beat himself up, give himself grace, and to consider hiring an executive coach to help him navigate the choppy waters of this new role.

Joel said he thought that was a good idea, and that he would think about it. But he said he wanted to *try to figure it out himself first*. Joel believed that hiring a coach was admitting failure and he perceived getting help was a sign he wasn't capable.

I explained to Joel that all of those things were actually true. ***He*** *was failing*, and *he wasn't capable*, currently, on his own and in his own capacity.

His pride was keeping him stuck. I reminded Joel that if he really wanted to succeed, that many answers and solutions were just one key person away who had more experience and wisdom than he did. Joel saw asking for help as a sign of weakness, when in actuality, it is the ***truest*** sign of strength. Joel politely passed on my suggestion and struck out on his own.

About a month later, I checked in on Joel and things were even worse. More sleepless nights, and now his job had begun affecting his marriage. Not only was work overwhelming, things were suddenly stressful at home too. I explained to Joel that he was on the cusp of something great. That he was growing, stretching, and evolving into a better leader and better CEO and that all the discomfort he was feeling was a good thing. He was experiencing a crucible of sorts that had an opportunity to shape him into his higher self. But I also reminded Joel he needed help and that he was at a crossroads; he could keep going on his own and likely implode on all levels, or simply just ask for help and likely succeed on all levels. After a long back and forth, Joel saw the simple logic and agreed to call a coach and ask for help.

Joel began working with a new coach and things began to slowly turn around. One key relationship, and Joel's life began to change. With a fresh set of eyes, greater wisdom, and new objectivity, Joel's role as the CEO began to get exponentially better. All because he was willing to step out of his comfort zone of self-sufficiency. ***Sometimes, asking for help is the hardest thing to do in getting off plateaus.***

Joel has since left that original company and has continued to thrive in his career, moving up, moving on, and moving higher into more prestigious and challenging roles. Joel has gone to the next level, and still works with his coach ten years later.

 So let me ask you: Who is going with you?

THE ACCOUNTABILITY EQUATION

In order to have a massively powerful Life-Team, we need to build something called the accountability equation. The accountability equation is when two or more allies on your Life-Team know everything and anything about you, including your hopes and dreams, your plans, and also your intimate struggles. **And those two or more allies also know each other.**

With the accountability equation, everyone knows everyone thus decreasing the likelihood for deception.

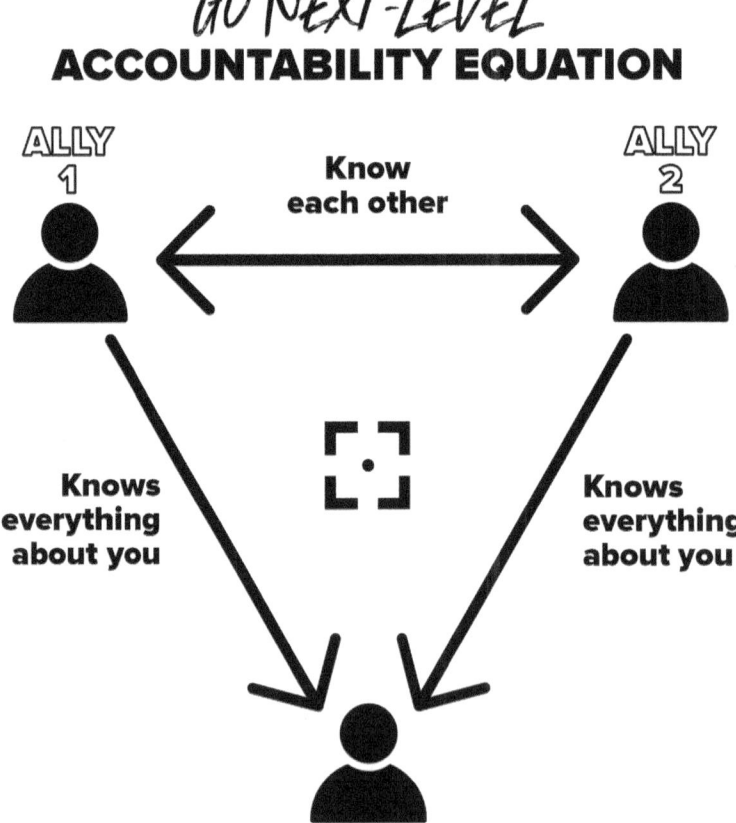

Many years ago, I realized my clients weren't always honest with me. Yes, that's right, even in a relationship that is built on trust, and intentionality, people still lie. I never judge people for not being honest, sometimes it's very challenging for different reasons to share difficult things. I get it. But we have to solve for it, because without full transparency, we'll be tempted to diminish the truth of our lives and businesses.

I coached a pastor at a church that was going through a potential divorce and it was having a ripple effect through the church leadership and congregation. My role in this pastor's life was to help him navigate the complexities of his looming divorce while maintaining his position of leadership at the church. The story I was given about the looming divorce was that the pastor's wife, having been married for twenty-five years, decided to end the marriage when the youngest child graduated high school and the couple became empty nesters. My client, the pastor, seemed shocked, heartbroken, and devastated about his wife's decision. We began working together on the messaging to the church and how we would articulate this bombshell of news so that it wouldn't devastate the church congregation.

Shortly into our working together, I learned the pastor and his wife were in marriage counseling prior to me coming on board to the assignment, and I asked the pastor if I could speak with the marriage counselor to better understand the marriage challenges they faced. I believed having all the details would help craft our messaging to the church. To my surprise, the pastor was resistant to the idea of me talking to the marriage counselor.

Instantly, alarm bells rang in my head. I knew he was lying to me and hiding something.

I explained to him that in order for me to adequately help him and help the church, I needed to understand the whole picture. He relented, and eventually agreed that I could speak with the marriage counselor, but before I even had a chance, he came clean. He revealed to me that the reason the marriage was ending was because he had a five-year affair with one of his assistants at the church. He didn't want me to talk with the marriage counselor because the marriage counselor would reveal that information.

Long story short, we navigated the complexities of this reality, created the appropriate messaging to the church, and helped the pastor transition in the best way possible. The moral to this story is that we all, including people held to high moral standards like pastors of churches, create different stories for different people as a way to preserve self-image, protect themselves, navigate sticky situations, and avoid painful realities. The accountability equation is a tool that reduces the likelihood of that happening.

Having a relationship of confidence with one person is not enough, we need to have a relationship of confidence with two or more people, who know each other. Essentially, this is ***true community***. And when it comes to elevating to the next level in life and business, we need to put everything on the table. Full transparency and no secrecy.

 So let me ask you: Do you have the accountability equation in your life?

ALL YOUR IDOLS HAVE A LIFE-TEAM

From all my experience, I've learned to predict who will be ultra-successful in life and business, and who will peak early, plateau and burnout, based on their understanding of a Life-Team. The people who rise fast, but are not able to sustain it for the long haul, never have a Life-Team and refuse to be open to one. Their pride can't handle it. And conversely, the people who build lives and businesses that we all admire, have learned to overcome the fears of transparency and vulnerability, and all have powerful Life-Teams. Here are some other tangible benefits when you have a true entourage of support in way of a Life-Team:

- **REMIND YOU OF YOUR WHY:** Life has many twists and turns along the way. If we don't have a Life-Team to continually remind us of our Big Why, we might lose sight of it and begin making decisions that take us off course. Your Life-Team helps keep the main thing, the main thing.
- **HOLD YOU ACCOUNTABLE:** We are all, at times, lazy people who are hard-wired to look for shortcuts and the paths of least resistance. We'll look to save calorie expenditure at any chance we get. Our Life-Team holds us accountable to doing the hard things we would rather avoid, knowing that doing those hard things keeps us headed in the right direction.
- **UNCOVER YOUR BLIND SPOTS:** There is a powerful cliche in psychology that says, "we don't know what we don't know." Having a Life-Team helps us see areas of our lives we're truly blind to. No amount of self-reflection illuminates areas of our lives like the power of another person who knows us well.
- **PRAISE YOUR WINS:** Equally as important as having someone challenge us, is having someone praise us when we get a win. It can feel lonely on your climb to the top, and we need a Life-Team to celebrate with us when we get wins, have successes, or cross pivotal milestones.
- **INTEGRATES THE PERSONAL WITH THE PROFESSIONAL:** Your Life-Team knows your family and the personal struggles you carry. Whether it is problems with addictive tendencies, physical health challenges, or problems in your home life to any degree, your Life-Team understands that any business success at the expense of a costly personal liability is never worth the trade off, and holds you accountable as such.
- **CHALLENGES YOUR MINDSET:** Your Life-Team often believes in you more than you believe in yourself. You have doubts, fears, and insecurities that will plague you and stop you from reaching your potential. Your Life-Team exists to challenge those limiting beliefs. Without the Life-Team, you'll reach only a small fraction of your capacity due to your limiting mindset.

The Life-Team concept has numerous benefits, but these are a few of the big ones. Remember, we're getting off plateaus and going to a whole new level, and we can't get there by ourselves. Plain and simple. You can get far on your own, but you simply can't reach the top of what is truly possible for you without the power of the Life-Team behind you.

 All your idols have a Life-Team. What is holding you back from emulating them?

YOUR PERSONAL BOARD OF DIRECTORS

David is a business-owner and a member of one of my mastermind groups. He owns a sales-training company for small to medium sized businesses, and was struggling to grow his business. It seemed like no matter how much money and time he threw at marketing and advertising, it wasn't translating to new clients. After hiring several marketing agencies with little success in changing the trajectory of his sales, I asked David if he could share his marketing plan, and any marketing materials with the mastermind team he was part of.

I knew the people in David's mastermind group could help him, because they *intimately knew him.* And I suspected it wasn't a marketing problem at all, but more of a David problem.

In a mastermind meeting that lasted ninety minutes, David shared his struggle to grow sales in his business and the challenges he was having, even after hiring several agencies to help him. The mastermind group tore through his marketing materials and found several clear and obvious challenges, that were more about **David's mindset** around his marketing, than the marketing itself. Without going into all the boring technical details, David was given three specific areas to change **which were all blind spots for David.** They challenged him to report back to the group in ninety days with feedback about what was working and what was still a challenge.

After the ninety days were up, David reported back to the group with incredible optimism, sharing that his company was getting so many leads for new business he needed to hire more people to fulfill the new requirements. This is the power of having a Life-Team; they saw his blind spots, the limitations in his mindset, and they saw things David could never see on his own. And they could provide business-altering feedback for course correction. In one ninety-minute meeting, David solved a riddle that he couldn't solve on his own, because people really knew David.

Don't get me wrong, sometimes the best money spent is hiring professional marketing agencies to help your business, but in this case, it was the blind spots in David himself that were holding him back, and not the marketing itself. The marketing agencies would never know David at this deep level, and thus could never solve for the real problem, beneath the problem. All the X,Y, Z strategies never worked. Only having a Life-Team made the difference.

There are too many stories like David's to share, where a Life-Team provided so much value that was simply not possible had the person been going it alone. In addition to thousands of stories of business success, the mastermind group component of a Life-Team has saved marriages, restored families, helped people curb drinking, transformed physical health, and a myriad of other life-changing results. All of these Life-Team miracles of change helped people to Go Next-Level that otherwise would not have happened without one.

In any business, the CEO is responsible for making day-to-day decisions to run the company, but the Board of Directors is the group of people that makes sure the CEO is on the right path and fulfilling the responsibility to manage the company optimally. The Board of Directors is the backstop, in case the CEO is making poor decisions. The Board of Directors has visibility into the strategy, the vision, the day-to-day operations, and the financial wellbeing of the company. In a healthy company, the CEO reports to the Board of Directors.

 **You are the CEO of your own life, but who do you report to? Who is your Board of Directors?**

SELF-SUFFICIENCY IS THE ENEMY OF GREATNESS

A Life-Team bridges the gap for people who are too reliant on individual efforts, which keeps them stuck and plateaued. The road to going to the next level in any domain in life or business will be mired with landmines along the way ready to sink the ship. But when we create a Life-Team that consists of coaches to help you with clarity, mentors to help you with strategy, and a mastermind group to help you with accountability, it's nearly *impossible to lose*. Rolled up together you have a Life-Team ready to launch you to the top.

The Life-Team concept is a crucial and necessary part of launching off the plateau and going to the next level because of your reliance on self-ambition, hard work, self-sufficiency, and discipline. *And in a strange twist of events, these are the same things that will keep you stuck on the plateau.* You can only go so far on your own before you need to rely on the perspective, insight, challenge, and accountability from other people to help you see what you cannot see on your own. We borrow the eyes, ears, experience, and collective wisdom of the right others to take us to the next level.

You can't do it by yourself.

GO NEXT-LEVEL ACTION STEP:

YOUR PERSONAL BOARD OF DIRECTORS

The Coach	The Mentor	The Mastermind Team

Remember, self-sufficiency is the enemy of greatness. Right now, before you move onto Chapter Seven, fill in the above table with five people from each section that could serve as potential candidates or resources for developing your own powerful Life-Team.

GO NEXT-LEVEL KEY-TAKEAWAYS

CHAPTER SIX: "Who is Going with You?"

→ We can't go to the next level alone. No matter how good we are, **we need others to be great.** If we want to Go Next-Level, and launch from any plateaus, we have to have a team of people in our lives that will challenge us, encourage us, support us, grow us, stretch us, and hold us accountable to move in the direction that matters to us.

→ On your own, **you're confined by the limitations** of your thinking, your imagining, your creativity, and your beliefs of what is possible for you.

→ It's only when you surround yourself with right other people who can **see what you cannot see** that you'll make it past stuck plateaus and fulfill what you want in life and business. This group of people we intentionally surround ourselves with is called our **Life-Team.**

→ Our Life-Team is our personal **Board of Directors** we intentionally and deliberately appoint to be the council of our lives.

→ A Life-Team consists of a mix of **three key relationships:**
  » **MENTOR:** A Mentor is someone in your specific industry who helps you grow with specific knowledge, expertise, and wisdom. The Mentor helps you with strategy.
  » **COACH:** A Coach is someone who helps you with objectivity and helps you with clarity.
  » **MASTERMIND GROUP:** A Mastermind Group is a peer group of like-minded individuals who share your value system. The mastermind group helps you with accountability.

→ The majority of people who feel stuck and plateaued are often living on their own **private island of isolation** and disconnection. They live here for **two reasons:**
   » **LACK OF AWARENESS:** They haven't understood the immense value of what having a Life-Team can do for them.
   » **LACK OF TRUST:** They have a hard time trusting other people and don't feel comfortable having others speak into their lives.

→ Without the intentional surrounding of the right others to help grow you, challenge you, stretch you, and help you think new thoughts, you will only grow to the level of your own capacity. The Life-Team concept challenges the **individualistic and self-sufficient mindset.**

→ In order to have a massively powerful Life-Team, we need to build something called the **accountability equation**. The accountability equation is when **two or more allies** on your Life-Team know everything and anything about you, including your hopes and dreams, your plans, and also your intimate struggles. And those two or more allies also know each other.

→ You can only go so far on your own before you need to rely on the perspective, insight, challenge, and accountability from other people to help you see what you cannot see on your own. We borrow the eyes, ears, experience, and collective wisdom **of the right others** to take us to the next level.

CHAPTER SEVEN

WHO DO YOU *THINK* YOU ARE?

GO NEXT-LEVEL BLUEPRINT STEP #7:
DEVELOPING AN UNSHAKABLE MINDSET

> If you hear a voice within you say 'you cannot paint,' then by all means paint, and that voice will be silenced.

VINCENT VAN GOGH

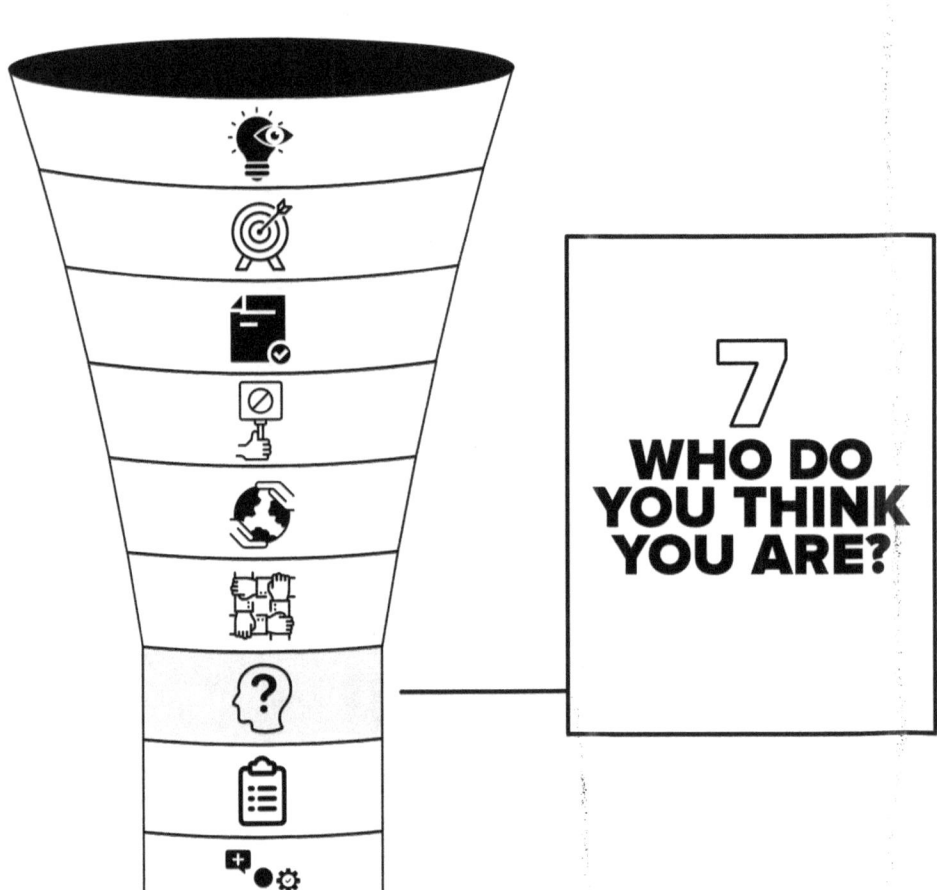

SUCCESS IS A DERIVATIVE OF SELF-BELIEF

So, truly, who do you *think* you are? Because how you think about yourself, your self-belief, and your identity will ultimately determine the level of success you'll be able to achieve. All of the planning, tactics, strategy, vision, the Big Why's, and the intentional surrounding yourself with key people will be limited or enhanced, depending upon the dialogue inside your own mind that tells you whether or not you're capable.

Our thoughts are the single most powerful aspect of our lives. Because ultimately, all of life, the good, the bad, and the ugly flows out of our thinking. To get to the next level we have to master our thought-life and the internal dialogue that tells us whether or not we are good enough, capable enough, smart enough, strong enough, or any other version of "enough" that will get in the way of launching off the plateau and soaring to the next level.

If you are stuck on a plateau, there's a good chance you don't *think* it's possible to move to the next level.

So let's ask this question again; "*Who do **you** think you are?*" I could think you are one of the most amazing and competent humans walking the planet, but at the end of the day, it's only who **you** think you are that really matters for going to the next level. It's your internal opinion of yourself informed by your accompanying thoughts of who you think you are that will either propel you toward the summit of life and business, or keep you stuck, unmotivated, uninspired, and surviving instead of thriving.

 To Go Next-Level, we have to cultivate a Go Next-Level Mindset.

Millions of people who are capable of world-shattering greatness never reach their full potential because they doubt what they are truly capable of. They doubt their capabilities and the value contribution they could create. It is this self-doubt, driven by often hostile and condemning internal thinking that comes from within, that keeps them from reaching their potential. Stuck on Early Peak Plateaus because they're not sure if they are worthy of getting unstuck.

EVERYTHING FLOWS OUT OF YOUR MINDSET

To get to the next level in life and business, you have to **begin to believe** you can actually reach your goals, dreams, and ambitions connected with your Ideal Life. If you're like many people who feel stuck on the plateau, there is that little voice inside your head that will tell you …

- » *I can't reach that goal without…*
- » *I don't have enough help to…*
- » *I'm not sure about…*
- » *I don't know how to do it…*
- » *It's too difficult…*
- » *I don't have the time….*
- » *No one has ever done that before…*
- » *This is a bad idea because…*
- » *I doubt anyone would agree…*
- » *They won't let us…*
- » *I can't…*

… or any number of self-limiting thoughts that will stop you on the path. Knowing how to silence those inner voices that tell you all the reasons you shouldn't pursue what's essential for you, is what separates people who remain on the plateau **wanting more**, and people who launch from the plateau and actually **get more**.

The Go Next-Level Mindset is the belief in ourselves that we are capable, competent, and deserving to pursue something that is deeply important. This is not the same as feeling entitled to something not earned. The Go Next-Level journey is developing master clarity about yourself, combined with a relentless dedication to break through barriers, which is the opposite of entitlement. But in order for you to reach great levels of success, you have to battle with the inner voices that will relentlessly try to take you off the path. As you battle, **and I mean battle**, with those critical inner voices that tell you all the reasons you shouldn't pursue what's possible, you begin to develop an unshakeable Go Next-Level Mindset.

Most likely, you don't have this kind of mindset. Not yet anyway, and that's okay for now. Very few people do. But over time, as you learn to challenge the limits in your thinking, the belief in yourself grows, and simultaneously your mindset changes in a way that will allow you to reach places you never thought possible.

> *"Whether you think you can, or you think you can't, you're right."*
>
> **HENRY FORD**

 To Go Next-Level, nearly everything about how we manage our thinking needs an upgrade.

SOWING SEEDS OF DOUBT

When I was a little kid, I wanted to own a donut shop. Like any little kid, I loved donuts and I loved going to the shop early on Sunday mornings with my dad. I loved watching the store owners make the donuts. I was a dreamer but my dad wasn't. He told me, *"That's crazy"* for wanting to own a donut shop. He explained to the eight-year-old me that there wasn't *"any good money"* to be made in a donut shop and that I was much better off doing something smarter. Doing something that would give me job security. And in a brief moment in time, with one interaction that was cemented into my memory, I stopped dreaming about being the donut shop owner. This was my dad, after all, and he certainly knew best. I learned in that little moment that a better path was to play it safe, and to avoid dreaming.

I don't judge my dad for saying these things, I see now this was his way of loving me and trying to *"talk sense into me"*. But I also know now that at some point in his own life, he had his own dreams too that he gave up on. **No little boy dreams of being a union worker**. But it was a paycheck, and health insurance, and my dad nobly raised his family in this profession, for which I am eternally grateful.

How many of us have big dreams but get talked into playing it safe? Someone told us the idea was "nuts", and this brought us crashing down to the *real world*. We started to doubt ourselves and second guess what was important to us. We started to doubt if we're capable. We started to doubt if we're smart enough. We started to doubt if we're good enough. We started to wonder if we're just too childish and immature for such a thing.

And then over time, our dream dies as all wonder and imagination is crushed by the doubt and uncertainty developing in our minds.

Most of us aren't lucky enough to grow up in families that encourage us to dream wildly. We don't grow up in families where the family narrative is that you can be and accomplish anything. That you can believe in yourself, fully. Most people develop scarcity mindsets because they grow up with parents that have scarcity mindsets. The way it goes in most families is that loving parents tell their children they are capable of great things, but this only lasts until the parent's fear gets activated when they see the child taking risks, and the messaging quickly turns from *"you can do anything"*, to *"make sure you're being safe"*. Without even knowing it, we have all been on the receiving end of someone sowing seeds of doubt in us. And then, without the help of anyone else, we sow our own seeds of doubt as we follow the conventional wisdom rooted in fear-based, and scarcity minded thinking.

To Go Next-Level, we're aiming for something big right? We're shooting for something spectacular, not just average. And with pursuing something big, we're going to be ***internally challenged*** by our existing mindset. ***The mindset that got us stuck on any plateau of life and business can not be the same mindset that carries us toward an Ideal Life.*** Our mindset has to change to Go Next-Level.

TACKLING THE INTERNAL JUDGE

When you think about getting unstuck from your plateau and going to the next level in life or in business, there is likely a little voice in the back of your mind that will tell you it's too ambitious, not achievable, selfish, or out of reach. That voice is part of your mindset. There are many names for this mindset, and I like to call it "The Judge". It's the voice of "reason" that is going to sentence you. This is not a nice judge, this is a judge that is going to convict you.

The Judge has been around for a long time; finding residence in your mindset in childhood. The Judge, although appearing to be an antagonist of your life, is actually not. The Judge has historically been your friend throughout life, psychologically protecting you from suffering defeat and experiencing rejection. This is the point of The Judge; to keep you from taking risks, so you don't experience psychological pain.

The internal Judge produces Judge-like thoughts in your mind to *protect* you from embarrassment, shame, rejection, and all other painful emotions that come when we take risks. The Judge has served you well and though you can honor The Judge for providing value in your life thus far, you must change your relationship with The Judge if you hope to Go Next-Level. The Judge, just like all psychological coping mechanisms, begins as a legitimate tool to protect your psychological well-being, and if not relinquished over time, ends up limiting you more than protecting you. The Judge, as part of your mindset, would be content with you metaphorically, safely locked in a prison cell.

Developing a Go-Next-Level Mindset is becoming aware of The Judge. We have to recognize when The Judge shows up in our life, when The Judge is speaking to us, and when The Judge is actively working against our plan to launch to new levels in life. The Judge is subtle, it whispers quietly things like:

"You can't do that..."
"No one has ever done that..."
"Don't you think that is excessive..."
"That seems selfish..."
"Do you really think you can do that?"

To Go-Next-Level, we have to develop insight and awareness into The Judge and learn how to replace and upgrade The Judge with a new mindset that will help us launch to new heights.

> *"Public opinion is a weak tyrant compared with our own private opinion."*
>
> **HENRY DAVID THOREAU**

THE #1 DIFFERENTIATOR BETWEEN SUCCESSFUL & UNSUCCESSFUL

The biggest determining factor that separates people who become ultra successful and reach massively ambitious goals and those who don't is that, at the end of the day, they believe in themselves. Successful people have doubts, insecurities, and limiting beliefs like anyone else, but they have a practiced ability to use tools and processes to overcome potentially derailing thought processes.

Unsuccessful people get stuck in those thought processes and progress gets halted.

 Although it seems astonishingly simple, the only thing standing between you and your goal is the story you tell yourself as to why you can't achieve it.

Simple, yes. Easy, no. Reaching the next level in life and business will require a conviction in your self-belief. If the belief in yourself is shaky, then your results will be shaky. To Go Next-Level and get unstuck from the plateau, we have to actually *think we can do it*. And this self-belief is the difference between those who launch from the plateau to greater heights, and those who stay stuck.

I remember a conversation I was having with my client Randy who was on the verge of divorce. His marriage was in shambles, and although in his heart of hearts he did not want to lose his marriage, he was ready to throw in the towel. In one of our conversations, I asked Randy how he *thought* of himself as a husband. He began by telling me all the things he did right, and the ways he was a good husband, and that he couldn't believe his wife didn't see all the great in him.

Not giving me the answer to my question, I asked him again, reminding him that I wasn't asking for him to tell me all the *behaviors* he did as a husband. I wanted to know what he *thought* of himself as a husband.

Randy paused, thought about the question for a good thirty seconds, and said, "*I think I am a failure*".

And so of course, he was in fact, failing. At the deepest level, despite his behaviors, he didn't see himself as capable of being successful. His innermost being, his subconscious belief, saw himself as a failure.

Steeped deeply in this self-destructive limiting belief as a husband, Randy experienced feelings of anxiety, anger, and shame when it came to his marriage. And no matter how much he tried to "behave well", or "do the right thing", it was all window dressing on the more true part of himself that believed he was a failure, which worked against his greater ideal of being successful in marriage.

In other words, his thoughts about himself as a failing husband actually produced a failing marriage.

And to make this point more broad, we can say it this way: ***our thoughts produce our realities.***

Cognitive Behavioral Psychology teaches us that **all** of human experience follows a predictive four-part pattern:

PART 1: We receive *stimulus* from the outside world.
PART 2: The stimulus produces a *thought* in our mind.
PART 3: The thought we have produces a *feeling* or emotional response.
PART 4: The emotional response produces a *behavior*.

This is what the four-part pattern looked like for Randy's marriage:

PART 1: *Stimulus:* Randy's wife gives him a *"dirty look"*
PART 2: *Thought:* *"She's always mad. I'll never get this right"*
PART 3: *Feeling:* Hopelessness / Anger / Shame
PART 4: *Behavior:* Randy internally shuts down, withdraws, and becomes reactive (but **tries** to be "good").

This was how Randy showed up in the marriage. All the "*good things*" he's doing are overshadowed by the real, deeper part of Randy, who was sure that he was a failure. I explained to Randy that if he really wanted to succeed and turn his marriage around, he would first have to start with changing his thoughts around his self-belief in his role as a husband. What if, instead of thinking, "*I can never get it right*", he started thinking, "*I **will** get it right, no matter what*". Because we have the power to challenge and change our

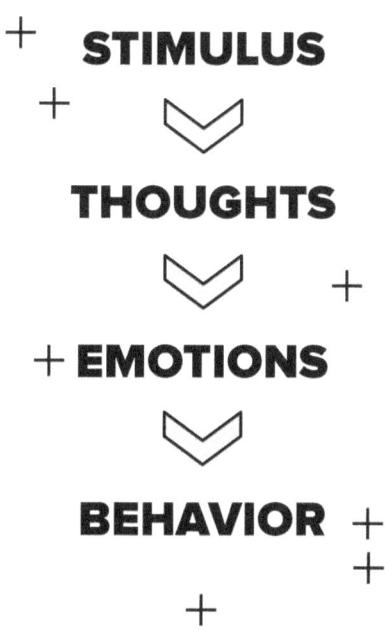

automatic thoughts, shifting our thinking in this way changes how we feel, which changes our behavioral responses.

Looking again at how all of life can be summarized into this four-part sequence, there are *two parts we can control, and two parts we have no control over*. Our thoughts and our behavioral responses are within our control. The stimulus from the outside world and the corresponding emotions we feel are not within our direct control.

Things we CAN control	Things we CAN NOT control
1. Thinking	1. Outside Stimuli
2. Behavioral Responses	2. Internal Emotions

Here is the best news in the world: We have control over our thinking, which changes how we feel. And as a result of changed emotions, we change our behavioral responses. The Go Next-Level Mindset is only possible when we understand the essentialness of human experience and that we have the ability and the need to take control of our thinking. ***Taking control of our thinking shapes the outcome of our realities.***

When we are on the journey to Go Next-Level, we will run into this four-part sequence, ***and we'll run into it every day.*** We will receive stimuli from the outside world, either confirming or denying our plans, and how we make sense of that stimulus with our thinking will shape how we feel, which will determine our outcomes. How we think about the stimulus we receive will either propel us toward something great, or it will keep us stuck on the plateau.

 It's not reality itself that keeps us stuck, it's how we think about reality that keeps us stuck.

Now, you might be thinking, "it can't be that simple!" It is, in fact, that simple, but it's not easy. It takes consistent effort, practice, and a commitment to change our habitual thinking. All of us have limiting self-beliefs from our childhoods embedded into our psychologies that require consistent practice and effort to change. To Go Next-Level and actualize your Ideal Life, you need to become the kind of person that believes you can actually get there. The story about Randy and his marriage can be applied to any part of your life; income levels, promotions, physical health goals, relationships, and anything you have stated important in your Ideal Life.

Examples of other self-limiting thinking that will stifle your Go Next-Level journey:

» *I can't reach that goal without…*
» *I don't have enough help to…*
» *I'm not sure about…*
» *I don't know how to do it…*

- » *It's too difficult...*
- » *I don't have the time....*
- » *No one has ever done that before...*
- » *This is a bad idea because...*
- » *I doubt anyone would agree...*
- » *They won't let me...*
- » *I can't...*

UNPACKING SELF-LIMITING THOUGHTS

Spend some time working through the below questions to help you assess where you're at with any plateau thinking, limiting beliefs, or self-defeating thoughts keeping you from reaching the summit of your own life. Whether it is a personal or professional vision for your Go Next-Level journey, you have to **radically** alter your thinking in order to get where you want to go.

- » If you are a parent, what aspirational things do you **think** about your children that you could also **think** about yourself?
- » What would life look like if you **thought** it could work?
- » Why do you **think** it couldn't work?
- » What would you **think** if it did work?
- » What if your life depends on **thinking** you can do it?
- » Where is your comfort zone in your **thinking**?
- » How are these self-limiting **thoughts** keeping you safe?
- » How are these self-limiting **thoughts** harming you?
- » What was reinforced in your limited **thinking** as a child?
- » Who do you **think** you are?
- » What would you **think** if you knew you couldn't fail?

A client of mine had a dream to charge $1,000/hour for her financial consulting services. When I asked her why she wasn't charging it now, she said, "*I could never charge that!*".

In asking her why she believed that, she told me:

She didn't *think* she was seasoned enough to charge these fees.
She didn't *think* people respected her enough to charge these fees.
She didn't *think* she was the kind of person who charged these fees.

All of this limited thinking had its roots in her family upbringing where people who made good money were perceived as "*greedy*" and "*selfish*". Her thoughts, her self-belief, and her identity didn't associate herself with $1,000/hour fees. This was what psychologists call cognitive dissonance. Where our thoughts (cognition) are incongruent with what is possible in reality (dissonance).

For her to become a $1,000/hour financial consultant, she needed to deconstruct her thinking and self-limiting beliefs around money. By changing her thinking, she began to see herself as a $1,000/hour financial consultant and beyond. With practice and a firm dedication to transforming her mindset around money, she slowly started to see herself as someone who made that kind of money. As of the writing of the page, she is well beyond the $1,000/hour mark and has created a 9-figure business. None of which would have been possible had she not destroyed old habitual limited thinking, and transformed it with a new way of looking at her relationship with money.

Whether it's setting higher fees, being successful in marriage, or reaching wild business goals, it all starts and ends with our thinking. It all starts and ends with whether or not we *believe* we actually have what it takes to get to where we want to go. Everything comes from our thinking. When we believe we can, we will. When we believe we can't, we won't.

DEVELOP A GROWTH MINDSET TO GET OFF THE PLATEAU

The Go Next-Level Mindset is a growth mindset in which you see yourself and your abilities through a ***lens of possibilities***. This isn't just positive thinking. This is possibility thinking, combined with hard work and dedication. When you develop a growth mindset and start seeing your life through a lens of possibilities, you won't see yourself as fixed or stuck, but instead, you'll see your current circumstances as the starting point. In a growth mindset, we see ourselves as expansive, resilient, and ready to stretch ourselves toward new possibilities.

Here is a quick chart to differentiate a Go Next-Level Mindset versus an average mindset.

The Go-Next-Level Mindset	The Average Mindset
Embraces challenges as the doorway toward leveling-up	Avoids challenges because defeat is imminent.
Perseveres in spite of setbacks	Gives in when they come up against hardship
Believes that people are full of untapped potential	Believes that destiny is fixed
Is inspired and motivated by the success of others	Feels insecure by the success of others
Wants to learn radical new ways	Believes they already know
Accepts and embraces criticism	Ignores or dismisses criticism

In order to reach your full potential, you *have to* develop a new Go Next-Level mindset. You have to challenge your limiting beliefs and limiting thoughts holding you back from getting what you ultimately want out of life. ***Just like developing a world-class physique, for you to develop a growth mindset, it requires practice, consistency, and dedication to build that "muscle".*** Here are five ways you can start developing your Go Next-Level mindset that are time-tested and used by the most successful people in the world.

THE TOP 5 WAYS TO BEGIN CULTIVATING A GO-NEXT-LEVEL MINDSET

1. Reflect on your failures:

In order to go to the next level, we have to be open and willing to acknowledge and identify our shortcomings. Everyone has them, so no shame and no blame for identifying the areas that need improvement. Go Next-Level people are always analyzing their shortcomings, so they can make improvements. Fixed-minded people are paralyzed with shame when you identify their shortcomings. Tonight, (and every night if you want to turn it into a habit),spend ten minutes journaling about the failures you experienced that day and how you can make improvements.

2. Celebrate the success of others:

Growth-minded people celebrate others' success, and fixed-minded people feel envious and insecure about the success of others. When we celebrate others' success, it changes the neural wiring in our brains with a bent toward success. When we celebrate the success of others, we find inspiration, and we begin to see it as a possibility for ourselves too. Every day, find an opportunity to congratulate someone, praise someone, compliment someone, or affirm someone you see doing something great for themselves.

3. Seek new challenges:

Reaching the highest summit in life is only possible when you stretch yourself and your comfort zone pursuing challenges that feel out of reach. We intentionally seek challenges and we recognize our natural temptation to stay in our comfort zones, but our comfort zones are the places that will lead to being stuck on the plateau, so if we want to go to go to next-level places, we have to look for the path that will stretch us, grow us, challenge us, and push us. Every day, pick one really hard thing that feels like a challenge and do it. It can be something as simple as not eating sugar that day, or challenging yourself to make fifty sales calls. Growth-minded people look for something difficult every day because this is how we grow.

4. Learn to love criticism

Fixed-minded people hate criticism. They will avoid it at all costs because it hurts their ego. Growth-minded people learn to love criticism. They deliberately seek it out because criticism is one of the most effective tools to help us sharpen our swords. When we realize the sting of criticism is only a passing feeling we learn to embrace it and reap the rewards that come from it. Criticism sharpens our sword and helps us level-up. We'll start going to the next-level when we see criticism as a free gift, and if anyone's willing to give it, welcome it. Make it a point to regularly ask your Life-Team to provide you with feedback, hard truths, and criticism on whatever it is you're working on. Use the information to keep growing and stretching toward the next level.

5. Change your language

The words we use carry a lot of power. Since our language is a byproduct of our thinking, we need to eliminate words from our vocabulary, such as, *"I can't"*, *"I'm not sure"*, *"I'm not ready for that"*, *"I don't know enough"*, or any other word or phrase that keeps us stagnate and stuck. The word we want to start using from this point forward is **"YET"**. *"Are you a millionaire? Not yet." "Do you have the skills to do that? Not yet." "Are you happy in your marriage? Not yet."* The word **YET** is your new best friend and it should be something you say regularly as a marker of your intentionality that you're on a path of growth.

Incorporate these five tools into your life today to start cultivating your Go Next-Level Mindset. Remember, **we will actually become our thinking**, so it's essential that we manage our thoughts, challenge our thoughts, and replace our thoughts with better thinking that serves us in moving toward greatness. 99% of the world will never accomplish what they are capable of because of their self-limiting thinking. ***Don't be your own worst enemy by allowing your thoughts to destroy your future.***

Align the belief in yourself with *your truest potential* and watch your life begin to change.

- *Pharmaceutical companies have shown us that placebos often have the same efficacy as the drug itself.*
- *Medical doctors know that patients will heal exponentially faster from physical injury if they think positively about their healing.*
- *The best coaches in the world know that an outcome of a game is won or lost in the locker room before players head into the game.*

 The bottom line: Our minds shape our realities.

This concept is difficult to grasp because it defies our traditional way of thinking about nature. You've been conditioned to believe the opposite; that your circumstances shape your thinking. But imagine all the possibilities when we start to see how the world really works; that our thinking shapes our realities.

SO MUCH FOR BEING "*IMPOSSIBLE*"

Prior to 1954, "reality" was that the four-minute mile was impossible to break. Everyone said it was impossible and unrealistic. But someone had a different thought that compelled him to break the world record. In May, 1954 Roger Bannister broke the four-minute mile. ***The record stood for just forty-six days before someone else broke it again.*** So much for an "impossible" four-minute mile.

Since that time, nearly 1,800 other runners have also broken the four-minute mile. Without question, I imagine Roger doubted himself along the way. He must have questioned himself thousands of times, wondering if he was even sane for trying. I imagine many of his friends and family also questioned him. But undoubtedly, Roger overcame his own limiting beliefs and corresponding fears, and he challenged the conventional wisdom of the naysayers too. He developed a new and different way of thinking that was rooted in imaginative possibilities, which produced powerful feelings of determination, and the outcome is cemented in history.

> *"The eyes of others our prisons; their thoughts our cages."*
> **VIRGINIA WOOLF**

Right now as you read this, you want something ambitious too. It may not be a world-record athletic title, but it's just as important to you. It might feel too out of reach and too "unrealistic" but it's not. This is the fork in the road for you; *Are you going to see your future with imaginative possibilities, or are you going to allow self-limiting beliefs to keep you stuck?*

To get off the stuck plateau you need to begin cultivating a Go Next-Level Mindset. Our minds are too powerful and if we don't manage our thinking along the way we won't be able to architect what we really want. We will be halted by our self-limiting beliefs, slowed by our "realistic" thinking, and the internal Judge will condemn us for even trying.

The good news is that all of our thinking, and all of our belief systems, and all of our mindsets are within our power to control. We are in complete control of how we want to perceive everything in life and the sooner we can take the reins of this reality, the more we're going to accomplish things we never thought possible.

GO NEXT-LEVEL ACTION STEP:

Grab your pen and journal and create two columns. On the left column, write down your top three limiting beliefs from the prior section in this chapter. In the right column, create a list of 25 corresponding and contrasting thoughts, filled with imaginative possibilities, that challenge those three limiting beliefs.

Limiting Beliefs	Contrasting Thoughts

GO NEXT-LEVEL KEY-TAKEAWAYS

CHAPTER SEVEN: "Who Do You Think You Are?"

→ How you think about yourself, your self-belief, and your identity will ultimately **determine the level of success** you'll be able to achieve. If you are stuck on a plateau, there's a good chance you don't think it's possible to move to the next level.

→ Our thoughts are the **single most powerful aspect of our lives**. Because ultimately, all of life, the good, the bad, and the ugly flows out of our thinking. To get to the next level you have to master your thought-life and the internal dialogue that keeps you stuck.

→ The Go Next-Level Mindset is the belief in ourselves that we are capable, competent, and deserving to pursue something that is deeply important.

→ When you think about getting unstuck from your plateau and going to the next level in life or in business, there is likely a little voice in the back of your mind that will tell you it's too ambitious, not achievable, selfish, or out of reach. That is **"The Judge"**.

→ The Judge is the **voice of "reason"** that is going to sentence you. This is not a nice judge, this is a judge that is going to keep you stuck.

→ To Go-Next-Level, we have to develop insight and awareness into The Judge and learn how to replace and upgrade The Judge with a new mindset that will help us launch to new heights.

→ The biggest determining factor that separates people who become ultra successful and reach massively ambitious goals and those who don't is that, at the end of the day, **they believe in themselves.**

→ Successful people have doubts, insecurities, and limiting beliefs like anyone else, but they have a practiced ability to use tools and processes to **overcome potentially derailing thought processes.** Unsuccessful people get stuck in those thought processes and progress gets halted.

→ Although it seems astonishingly simple, the only thing standing between you and your goal is the **story you tell yourself** as to why you can't achieve it.

→ Cognitive Behavioral Psychology teaches us that all of human experience follows a predictive **four-part pattern:**

» **PART 1:** We receive stimulus from the outside world.
» **PART 2:** The stimulus produces a thought in our mind.
» **PART 3:** The thought we have produces a feeling or emotional response.
» **PART 4:** The emotional response produces a behavior.

→ There are two parts of human experience we can control, and two parts we have no control over. **Our thoughts and our behavioral responses are within our control.** The stimulus from the outside world and the corresponding emotions we feel are not within our direct control.

→ The Go Next-Level Mindset unlocks when we understand that we have the ability and the need to take control of our thinking. Taking control of our thinking shapes the outcome of our realities.

→ Because it's not reality itself that keeps us stuck, **it's how we think about reality** that keeps us stuck.

→ The Go Next-Level Mindset is a growth mindset in which you see yourself and your abilities through a lens of possibilities. This isn't just positive thinking. **This is possibility thinking**, combined with hard work and dedication.

→ Our minds are too powerful and if we don't manage our thinking we won't be able to architect what we really want. We will be halted by our self-limiting beliefs, slowed by our "realistic" thinking, and the internal Judge will condemn us for even trying.

→ The good news is that all of our thinking, and all of our belief systems, and all of our mindsets **are within our power to change.**

CHAPTER EIGHT

WHAT IS THE PLAN?

GO-NEXT-LEVEL BLUEPRINT STEP #8:
GETTING LASER FOCUSED WITH
GO NEXT-LEVEL GOALS

> If you're bored with life – you don't get up every morning with a burning desire to do things – you don't have enough goals.
>
> LOU HOLTZ

THE GO NEXT-LEVEL BLUEPRINT

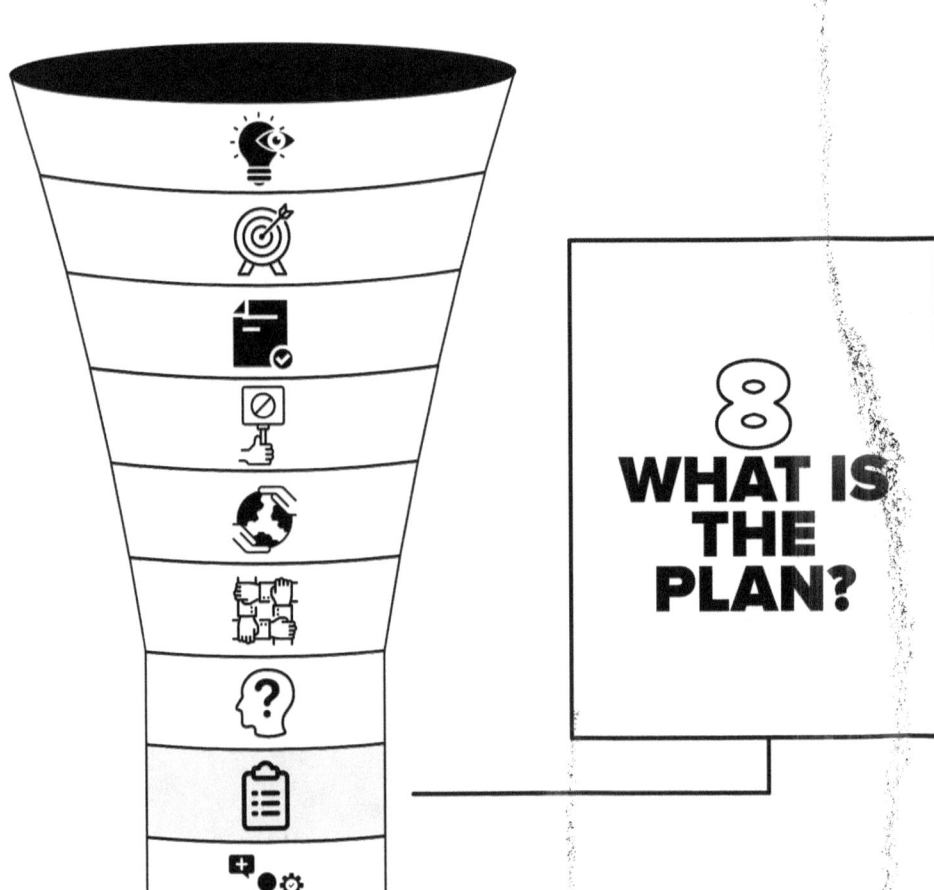

8
WHAT IS THE PLAN?

AMBITION WITHOUT GOALS IS JUST A WISH

"*Your goals suck.*"

That was my response to my friend who just shared his goals with me. He and I have the kind of friendship where we can be open and direct with each other, so I didn't hold back.

I said to him, "*These goals are not impressive. If these were my goals, I'd just want to lay in bed all day because they are so boring and uninspiring. Are they **truly** inspiring to you?*"

He responded with, "*I mean ... kind of ... No, but they're attainable.*"

I replied, "*Working toward attaining something that is uninspiring is the surest way to live an unexciting life.*"

Going to the next level in life and business requires **massive amounts of clarity** about what it is that we actually want, which is what we discussed in Step One in the Go Next-Level Blueprint. Knowing what we want is the vision that keeps us focused on the path ahead. But in order to actualize that vision, we need to set bite-sized, actionable targets, to aim at along the way. These targets we're shooting at are clearly defined goals. And to get unstuck from the plateau and go to new heights in life and business, we have to incorporate the power of goal-setting.

But not just any goals. We need Go Next-Level type of goals.

Having clearly defined goals takes your ideas, visions, dreams, passions, and ambitions, and says, "OK, *now let's get serious about all of this and start building.*" **Big dreams without clearly defined and actionable goals are just wishes that will never come to fruition.**

Goals become the container we place all of our dreams. Goals become something manageable we can work toward and achieve, and not just dream about.

I can always tell how far someone is going to go by understanding their relationship to goals. In first conversations with people, I always say, "Send me your goals ahead of our first meeting so I can see what you're working on." Sometimes, people shoot their goals over to me right away, and sometimes people say, "Give me a few days and I'll put something together to send to you." The person with the goals ready to go is always ten steps ahead of the person who doesn't have them.

Goals keep you focused, and when done right, goals become the blinders you wear, tuning out everything else in life that is irrelevant and keeping you away from the essentials. Goals have never been more critical for people who want to go to ultra-high places in life and business. We live in a hyper-distracting world with a million competing interests pulling at our attention. From other people wanting something from us, to social media, to the news playing while you're pumping gas, everyone and everything is trying to grab your attention. You cannot let them.

According to research on goal-setting, only about 20% of the American population sets goals. And of the 20% who do set goals, only about 30% of that group of people will succeed in achieving their goals. Said another way, about 6% of the population achieves their goals.

If we only looked at goal-setting behavior and those who accomplish their goals, we could say that at most, 6% of the population could be considered on the Go Next-Level path, but even that number is too high. Because many people, even those who accomplish their goals, are accomplishing goals that are barely important to them. They don't have clarity about their Ideal Life, there's no Big Why, they're not clear on their Million-Dollar Mission, and therefore, the goals they set are flat, boring, and uninspiring. Their goals become nothing more than a task list.

Traditional goal-setting gurus said that some people don't accomplish their goals because their goals are too ambitious. This is rarely the case. **Most people are afraid to create lofty goals, so they create goals that are "achievable" and "realistic", but fail to reach them because the goal itself wasn't inspiring enough to work toward.** Human beings are reasonable creatures; we're not going to work hard on something that doesn't inspire us. We need goals

STATISTICS ON GOAL-SETTING IN AMERICA

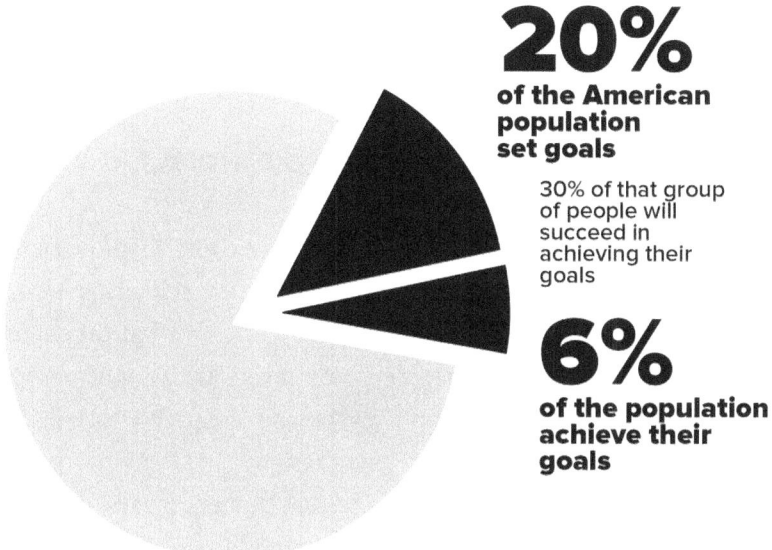

20% of the American population set goals

30% of that group of people will succeed in achieving their goals

6% of the population achieve their goals

that frighten us. In a good kind of way. Because if your goals don't frighten you, they're probably not worth pursuing.

If you're one of the people reading this now and do set goals, are they massively inspiring to you? Or, are your goals so boring the thought of pursuing them puts you to sleep? Great goals need to inspire you deeply. Great goals need to be something that freak you out and send adrenaline coursing through your veins. They need to be something that makes you nervous. If your goals don't feel this way, your motivation to achieve them will fizzle. Why would anyone work hard to accomplish something they aren't passionate about? I wouldn't. Neither would you.

This is why 70% of goal-setters never reach their goals. Not because they were too much, but because they were too little. To Go Next-Level, we have to set different kinds of goals from what you've been traditionally taught.

> "The size of your dreams must always exceed your current capacity to achieve them. If your dreams don't scare you, they aren't big enough."
>
> **ELLEN JOHNSON SIRLEAF**

GOALS TRANSFORM DREAMS INTO TANGIBLE ACCOMPLISHMENTS

If you talk to most people about what they are working on or what they are trying to accomplish in their lives, they will likely give you a vague and unclear answer. Very few people know what they actually want, and since most people don't have clarity about what's important to them, they haven't crystalized the path to get there with laser-focused, awe-inspiring, and tangible goals. Without the focus that goals provide, your day-to-day existence usually turns into a fuzzy and murky mess of thoughts and ideas that keep you stuck on the plateau and out of reach of your truest potential.

Before I had kids, I had the luxury of lots of free time that I used to train for triathlons. I love endurance training and the opportunity to be with myself in solitude putting my body through tough physical tests. I always **had a desire** to complete an Ironman distance race. Ever since I was young, I knew I wanted to do an Ironman race. It had always been a thought in the back of my mind that one day, I would love to accomplish. I remember watching an Ironman race taking place in Hawaii on television and thinking these guys and gals were absolute superheroes for accomplishing this incredible endurance feat.

But here was the problem: doing an Ironman distance race was just a dream, but not a goal. It was an ambition, but not a goal. It was a desire, but not a goal. It was steeped in intention, but I hadn't solidified it into a true goal, and therefore, I would not move any closer to truly accomplishing it.

One day, serendipitously, I was introduced to a veteran Ironman athlete who coached people with endurance training, and in our first interaction, she asked me, "*What are your goals?*"

I gave her the same vague answers about this and about that, that I had been repeating in my own mind for several years, and I knew as soon as the words left my mouth, it wasn't a good answer for her. She reflected on my words for less than 3 seconds, and in typical coach fashion, she said, "*you'll **never finish** something as hard as an Ironman with such weak goals.*"

As much as I didn't want to admit it, I knew she was right. And in this moment, I had to make a decision; I was either going to make my dream of doing an Ironman a reality, or I was going to let the dream keep dying in my mind day after day. I decided that life was too short to let my dreams die, and so I asked her to help me. And over the next hour she made me commit to defining the scary and nerve-wracking goal to complete an Ironman race that was only five months away. Now it was real. No more dreaming. I was committed.

The Goal: Finish Ironman St. George Utah on May 12, 2012.

Because the goal was clear, and quite scary, I couldn't slack off. I only had five months to train, which is quite a short window to train for a 2.4 mile swim, a 112 mile bike ride, and a 26.2 mile run, all in the same day. Appropriately freaked out by my new goal, along with new accountability meetings, I rigorously followed the training schedule she planned for me to make sure I was on track.

On May 12, 2012, I crossed the finish line at Ironman St. George, Utah. Prior to this day, it was just a fun dream and hazy ambition. Because of an actionable, scary, and clearly defined goal, my fun dream and hazy ambition became a milestone accomplishment.

 This is the power of goals: They take dreams otherwise likely to die, and turn them into accomplished realities.

As humans, we wrongly trust that our desire and motivation will be enough to take us to far places. But it won't. Ambition is easily lost. Motivation wanes like the blowing wind. We trust too much that our ambition and desire will help us accomplish great things, but those emotions will always leave us feeling let down. We need to harness our ambition into a crystallized form, which is the power of clear and inspiring goals. Prior to my Ironman goal, I only had an ambition and it was getting me nowhere. Once it was cemented into a clear goal, there was no turning back and it produced my desired outcome.

Be skeptical of your own motivation and ambition. If your motivation and ambition is not attached to actionable goals, you will be let down and stuck on plateaus. Only with Go Next-Level Goals, will you launch to unimaginable accomplishments.

GOALS GIVE US ACTIONABLE CLARITY

This section of the Go Next-Level Blueprint is for the dreamers and the imagineers who are great at big ideas, but struggle with taking those big ideas and distilling them down into an actionable plan. Many people in life have big dreams, but it's only those who can take those big dreams and convert them into bite-sized actional steps that will result in success. Our minds need to strike that balance between dreaming big, and also simply putting one foot in front of the other. As illustrated in the diagram on the next page, the Go-Next-Level Blueprint starts wide, and becomes increasingly narrow by creating actionable steps to help us in launching to unprecedented places.

Rick, one of my clients, was great at dreaming big. Every time he and I talked about what he wanted in the future, I was always personally inspired. His creativity, outside-the-box thinking, and his vision for the future was always impressive. It was part of Rick's Ideal Life to become the CEO of this company. This was Rick's getting off his own plateau and going to the next level.

THE *GO NEXT-LEVEL* BLUEPRINT

1. WHAT DO YOU WANT?

2. WHY DO YOU WANT IT?

3. WHAT DO YOU NEED TO SAY "YES" TO?

4. WHAT DO YOU NEED TO SAY "NO" TO?

5. HOW ARE YOU GOING TO SAVE THE WORLD?

6. WHO IS GOING WITH YOU?

7. WHO DO YOU THINK YOU ARE?

8. WHAT IS THE PLAN?

9. HOW ARE YOU GOING TO GET THERE?

So Rick and I worked to create some actionable goals to make this a reality for him that included key-relationship building, leadership skill development, influential networking, and joining projects that would get him continual exposure to the C-suite and Board of the company he worked for. Rick had a solid plan to Go Next-Level, he just needed to execute it.

But there was the problem with Rick: every time he and I would talk about his progress in working towards his goals, he would tell me how he was getting derailed with a new idea, and distracted working on a new exciting project, and for a myriad of dreamy reasons, he wasn't moving toward his goals. After this kept going on and on for nearly six months, I explained to Rick that he would never become CEO if he continued to lose focus of his goals. Rick was distracted, regularly off-course, and scattered. As long as he didn't stick to working on his goals with a disciplined fervor, he would spin his wheels and wouldn't discover the freedom he wanted from his own plateau.

Rick needed the structure of goals to stay on track, but at the same time, loathed the discipline required to stay on target. His lofty ambition and big dream mindset was a huge asset for Rick, but it was also his Achilles heel too. He had a case of creative and ambitious ADD.

And this is the challenge about goals for some people; they move us out of dreaming into actionable doing. And for some this feels boring. **And the truth is, the routine day-in and day-out working toward the same goal until you accomplish it, is often quite boring.** In that state of boredom, it's easy to get sidetracked by a shiny object, no matter how bad you might want to reach your dream.

Staying committed to goals are the fruits and veggies version of your aspirational life. Disciplined commitment provides the essential nutrients, but isn't as much fun to eat. We need this discipline, but avoid it because it doesn't give us the *dopamine rush* like other things will. But without these nutrients of clear goals, pursued with discipline, we will never Go-Next-Level and launch from the plateau.

This step in the Go Next-Level Blueprint is necessary because it highlights and confronts the dreamers from the reality makers. When we take all of our dreams and ambitions and put them into actionable goals, we immediately separate ourselves from the masses who dream but will never do. Dreaming is great, but if it doesn't make its way from the dream into an actionable plan, the dream dies in our hearts. Creating clear and actionable goals that are attached to what is most meaningful to us separates the people who remain stuck on the plateau from those who **actually** launch to a new level and fulfill great things.

 Goals take what is unseen and make it seen. Goals take the invisible and make it visible.

The Ideal Life you are architecting in Chapter One is not easy to reach. Impossible to reach without goals. Goals become the activating ingredient that puts the wheels into motion on a *practical path* toward the Ideal we're striving for.

GOALS TAKE THE INVISIBLE AND MAKE IT VISIBLE

The success of your Go Next-Level journey is dependent on your relationship and behavior with goals. And, you won't be able to get off the plateau and rise to new levels without clear goals. Take a look at the below questions to give yourself an assessment of where you are with your own goal setting process:

» Do I have my goals written down somewhere I can easily access and review?
» Do I review my goals on a minimum of a weekly basis?
» Are my goals challenging enough to feel anxiety provoking?
» Are my goals ambitious to the point of being unrealistic?
» Are my goals attached to the Ideal scenario I outlined in Chapter One?

- » Are my goals attached to my Mission and how I'm going to save the world?
- » Have I shared my goals with a supportive accountability system, i.e. Life-Team?
- » Do my goals have hard timelines attached to them?
- » Do my goals support my desired legacy and how I want to be remembered?
- » Do my goals make me a better person and those around me?

Goals are not the same as task lists. We might have task lists that support reaching our goals, but goals are tangible targets and milestones where we can measure our progress. For example, one of my goals is to get my black belt in BJJ twenty-four months from now. My task list includes training, teaching classes, workouts, and all the things I must do in order to reach the goal of getting my black belt. In twenty-four months, I will either have my black belt or I won't. It's clear, time bound, and measurable.

Chances are, you've heard of SMART goals. But before you consider closing the book here due to a topic you've heard 1,000 times, stay with me for a minute. The SMART acronym is important, ***but it's just the beginning***. Just a reminder about SMART goals:

- **(S) SPECIFIC:** My goal is to get my black belt. It's specific. It's not a goal to "get better at BJJ" because that wouldn't be specific and tangible enough to know whether or not I've accomplished the goal.
- **(M) MEASURABLE:** All goals need to be measurable. If I get my black belt, that is something measurable, and if I don't, that is also measurable.
- **(A) ACHIEVABLE:** If I were a blue belt, it would be mostly impossible to get my black belt in twenty-four months, so when we set goals, we want to make sure we're setting goals that are actually attainable.

(R) RELEVANT: Setting goals not relevant to what is important to us will leave us with accomplishments that don't matter. We don't need any of those. Great goals have to be relevant to what is most important to us.

(T) TIME-BOUND: All great goals need to be time-bound and have a completion date. Open-ended goals that are not time-bound will result in unfinished and half-finished accomplishments.

Using the SMART acronym to create your goals is a time-tested system that will keep you focused, on-track, and provides an easy framework to make sure you can take all your desires and convert them into actionable goals that will help you get to where you want to go.

But SMART goals are just the beginning. Our goals also need to be SUPER.

Because SMART goals by themselves typically don't leave people feeling inspired and ready to put a dent in the universe. Every goal you create should also pass the SUPER test:

(S) SCARY: Your goals have to scare you. If they don't, it just means you're playing too small and dreaming too little. Your goals need to give you a nervous sense of excitement and an uneasy feeling about sharing your goals with other people. That's how you know you're chasing Go Next-Level goals.

(U) UNIFYING: Your goals need to integrate all aspects of your life, holistically. Humans are finely-tuned machines and if we are out of balance, we'll experience significant challenges. Make sure your goals are integrating every important aspect of your life; personal, professional, relational, and spiritual. If we pursue one goal at the expense and harm of other aspects of our life, it will throw the system out of harmony and leave you unaccomplished and unfulfilled.

- **(P) PURPOSEFUL:** Too often, people pursue goals not connected to their Big Why or their Million-Dollar Mission. And then, of course, the goal dies because it hasn't been attached to something deeply meaningful and eternally important. Make sure your goals are connected with your greater calling on earth.
- **(E) ENERGIZING:** If your goals drain your energy, they are the wrong goals. Your goals need to energize you and make you want to jump out of bed and pursue them. When our goals are right, they always give us mountains of enthusiastic energy for tackling them.
- **(R) RIDICULOUS:** Our best goals should make us laugh a little. The SMART goal setting system says we need to be realistic, but there is a problem with being realistic; it's not exciting and therefore not captivating enough to pursue with fervor. Every goal that I've accomplished that has really mattered to me felt unrealistic when I set it. The ridiculous aspect of SUPER goals have stretched me into a realm I didn't think was possible.

Don't be lulled to sleep by only using the SMART acronym for your goal-setting. Make sure you're taking things to a moderately insane new level by running all your goals through the SUPER acronym too. *Remember, most people fail to accomplish their goals not because they are too ambitious, but because they are not ambitious enough.* Goals that don't excite are not worth pursuing. This is Go Next-Level goal-setting.

GIVING YOURSELF THE BEST SHOT AT MAKING YOUR GOALS A REALITY

In addition to running your goals through the SMART and SUPER acronyms, there are some other tried and true fundamentals when it comes to goal setting that will exponentially increase your likelihood of accomplishing your Go Next-Level goals. Because what is the point of having great goals if you don't have a proven system for making sure you accomplish them? Go one step further past simply the creation of your goals and apply the proven principles on goal-setting to give yourself the best shot at getting them over the finish line.

When it comes to Go Next-Level goal-setting, there are five proven applications that we must apply to make sure we're accomplishing our goals that will take us off any stuck plateaus.

1. Write your goals down on paper
2. Don't set more than five goals at a time
3. Create an actionable plan to accomplish your goals
4. Make your goals visible so you can review them often
5. Create accountability around your goals

1. Write your Go Next-Level Goals down on paper

If they're not written down, you have a small likelihood of accomplishing them. If they are not written down somewhere they're just ideas and thoughts in your mind that will be quickly forgotten and mentally crowded out by other important things in your life. Research on goal-setting from the University of California found that participants were 42% more likely to accomplish their goals when they were written down. *There is magic that happens when we put our goals into writing; they become real. If your goal is not written, it's no goal at all.*

2. Don't set more than five Go Next-Level Goals at a time

People with too many goals become confused and scattered. We lose focus. Having more than five active goals ends up creating an environment where there are too many competing interests with your different goals and you're likely to accomplish none at all.

3. Create an actionable plan to accomplish your Go Next-Level Goals

Dreams without goals are just fun ideas, and goals without actionable plans are just wishes. Once we have our goals established, we need to create an actionable plan around the goals. We'll talk more about this specifically in the last chapter on Go Next-Level Habits, but for now, just remember that goals will never come to fruition unless we create a specific plan to achieve the goal. Research has shown that people who create an actionable plan around their goals generate 40% more progress in reaching their goals than those who don't create a plan.

4. Make you Go Next-Level Goals visible so you can review them often

Look at your goals at least once per week. Why? Because out-of-sight means out-of-mind. You will forget what you are working on and need a continual reminder of the lane you are trying to stay in. It's too easy to get side-tracked on a million other important projects that will take you off course from your most important goals. If you don't review your goals often, you will not accomplish them.

5. Create accountability around your Go Next-Level Goals

Data on goal setting suggests the chance of achieving your Go Next-Level Goals increases by 65% when you include accountability into your goal-setting process. *If you want to Go Next-Level, you have to incorporate your Life-Team into your goal-setting process.* SUPER goals are not easy to accomplish, and if you're trying to accomplish goals in isolation, by yourself, you'll never make it. Accountability is the turbocharger you need to make sure you stay focused week in and week out to get your most important Go Next-Level goals over the finish line and launch to new heights.

THE MASSIVE HIDDEN BENEFITS OF GO NEXT-LEVEL GOALS

The creation of Go Next-Level Goals moves us out of the dreaming phase of the Go Next-Level Blueprint and into the tangible and concrete. This is essential for getting off the plateau and going to higher levels. All of the great people in history set goals. All of the ultra high-achieving people set goals. If we want to play a different game ourselves, we need to take a play out of the book of greats and become goal-junkies ourselves. There are numerous tangible and intangible benefits to the goal setting process in the Go Next-Level Blueprint, but let's outline the major ones to connect how important Go Next-Level Goals are to becoming your optimal self and reaching your optimum state.

Go Next-Level Goals will dramatically increase your performance

Having SUPER goals that excite and captivate us will elevate our level of performance. If we want to perform at the highest level, we need to continually be stretching ourselves to higher and higher standards, and we do this through Go Next-Level goal-setting. As the cliche goes, we don't rise to our standards, but fall to the level of our training. Working toward goals is the training we do day in and day out to continue growing, stretching, and raising our standards, which overtime, dramatically elevates our performance. For example, if your income is $1M per year and you set a goal to make $10M in two years, you will have to dramatically *elevate your performance* to achieve that goal. ***The goal itself will force you to look at your strengths, your weaknesses, and the areas you need to grow in order to add enough value to justify 10X'ing your income.*** Go Next-Level Goals have a powerful way of elevating our performance for *who we need to become* to reach our potential.

Go Next-Level Goals will exponentially increase your energy levels

When we're working on things that excite us, we have boundless energy. Conversely, when we're working on things that we're not passionate about, we will feel drained and our energy levels take a nosedive. When we're working toward ambitious and life-changing Go Next-Level Goals we'll rarely feel tired. People who feel flat, lethargic, depressed, and low-energy might find within themselves that they are really not working toward exciting life-changing goals. If you have goals, but you still feel low-energy, chances are the goals you're working toward aren't SUPER. Find the right goals, and you'll find a secret energy reservoir.

Go Next-Level Goals will tackle any sign of "laziness"

Reaching the Go Next-Level summit requires discipline. There is no getting around the fact that it takes effort and hard work. But for many people, they struggle with the required discipline to follow through with reaching their goals, not because they are lazy and unmotivated, but because they are not working toward goals that enliven them. When we have Go Next-Level goals, discipline gets easier and easier. If you look at your life and you have things unfinished or unaccomplished, chances are you're not lazy, you've been working on the wrong things. Because when we're working on *what's right for us*, discipline gets easier and easier.

Go Next-Level Goals will boost your self-confidence

There is no better way to skyrocket your self-confidence than to accomplish a powerful Go Next-Level Goal. Accomplishing goals creates a sense of personal mastery in your life that no one can take from you. You will feel competent and accomplished. You will develop an inner pride because you're able to do hard things and accomplish something difficult. By doing this, there's an incredible boost to your self-confidence and self-worth. If your confidence is lacking, work toward an exciting Go Next-Level Goal and commit to yourself that you will die before you accomplish this goal. Watch your self-confidence skyrocket and your life change.

Go Next-Level Goals will give you laser focus and clarity

When we have Go-Next-Level Goals we're working toward, we gain a massive amount of clarity and focus around how we spend our time. The world is bombarding us with thousands of distractions every day. Your email inbox is filled with useless junk vying for your attention. The apps on your phone are notifying you about time-sucking trivialities that will not improve your life by one degree. When we create the right goals, they become like blinders in our lives. These blinders block out everything that distracts us from the goal, and the goal itself becomes the tool that gives us focus and clarity. If we don't know exactly what we're working toward with precise clarity, *everything feels urgent and important.* If you struggle with shiny-object syndrome, there's a good chance you don't have crystallized goals.

GO-NEXT-LEVEL GOALS MOVE US PAST PLATEAUS

When I first met Dan, he was bored, depressed, hated going to work most days, and was making $6M a year as a partner of a large national accounting firm. He had more money than he needed, wasn't motivated by making more money, and his life had become unfulfilling. He needed help figuring out why his life wasn't working.

In our first conversation, Dan told me how he had grown the company over the last ten years and that he was very proud of his success. But he also explained to me that despite his abundance of financial success, he had lost his drive and enthusiasm for work. I congratulated him for his achievements. He had built something great and should be proud. I also empathized with him for spending so much of his life, time, and energy creating something he wasn't fulfilled by.

I asked Dan to show me the goals he was working toward that

year, and in our next meeting he brought lots of papers with graphs, spreadsheets, business planning documents, etc. that outlined his company's growth strategy. Dan told me that he was on plan to grow the company's revenue by 30%, and I asked him if that goal was something he woke up every morning excited to achieve. He said, "*I dread coming to work most mornings....*" My next logical question to Dan was, "*Why are you working so hard to achieve something that doesn't matter to you?*"

 Dan was caught in a common trap; continuing to do more of what you already know you don't want.

Dan struggled to think outside the box in ways other than revenue growth. I explained to Dan that more is **only better** if getting more also means more joy, more enthusiasm, more freedom, and more excitement. If it's not more of those things too, why would you pursue it?

Dan and I worked to create exciting new Go Next-Level goals that got him to spring out of bed in the morning to get building. Over the course of time, Dan began reorganizing parts of his life at home and his role in the company. He started to open up pathways for him to do things that excited him again. With new Go Next-Level Goals that centered around his Ideal Life, Dan found his zest for living again. For many years, Dan was chasing **empty and life-draining goals**.

I met Dan on a common plateau that many people hit; In the beginning of the career journey, you're driven by financial gain, then you reach a plateau where financial freedom has been achieved, but you struggle to construct meaningful goals other than more financial freedom. So you keep chasing more money hoping the spring in your step comes back like it once did, but it never does.

The plateau can never be overcome by the same thing that caused it.

Getting off the plateau always requires new ways of thinking, new ideas, and new ways of looking at the world and your life and business in it.

 The fastest way to living a miserable life is by doing more of what contributes to the misery.

GO NEXT-LEVEL ACTION STEP:

Grab your pen and your journal and create five goals right now that you would like to accomplish in the next twenty-four-months. Run the five goals through both the SMART and SUPER acronym. Consider reviewing Chapter One and your Ideal Life when you craft these five Go Next-Level Goals. Delay moving on to Chapter Nine until you've got these written down. Remember, they don't have to be perfect, you just have to get started. No more goals that don't work. No more goals that don't excite. No more goals that have us chasing things that are less than optimal.

GO NEXT-LEVEL KEY-TAKEAWAYS

CHAPTER EIGHT: "What is the Plan?"

→ In order to actualize our Ideal Life vision, **we need to set bite-sized, actionable targets,** to aim at along the way. These targets we're shooting at are clearly defined goals.

→ To get unstuck from the plateau and go to new heights in life and business, we have to incorporate the power of goal-setting. But not just any goals. We need Go Next-Level **SUPER goals.**

→ Having clearly defined goals takes your ideas, visions, dreams, passions, and ambitions, and says, "OK, now let's get serious about all of this and start building." Big dreams without clearly defined and actionable goals **are just wishes** that will never come to fruition.

→ Goals become the **container we place all of our dreams.** Goals become something manageable we can work toward and achieve, and not just dream about. Goals take what is unseen and **make it seen.** Goals take the invisible and **make it visible.**

→ Goals have never been more critical for people who want to go to ultra-high places in life and business because **we live in a hyper-distracting world** with a million competing interests pulling at our attention.

→ According to research on goal-setting, only about 20% of the American population sets goals. And of the 20% who do set goals, only about 30% of that group of people will succeed in achieving their goals. Said another way, **about 6% of the population achieves their goals.**

→ Traditional goal-setting gurus said that some people don't accomplish their goals because their goals are too ambitious. This is rarely the case. Most people are afraid to create lofty goals, so they create goals that are "achievable" and "realistic", but fail to reach them because the goal itself wasn't inspiring enough to work toward. Remember, the plateau **can never be overcome** by the same thing that caused it.

→ Great goals need to inspire you deeply. Great goals need to be something that freak you out and send adrenaline coursing through your veins. They need to be something that makes you nervous. If your goals don't feel this way, your motivation to achieve them will fizzle.

→ SMART goals are just the beginning. Our goals also need to be SUPER. Because SMART goals by themselves typically **don't leave people feeling inspired** and ready to put a dent in the universe.

→ Every goal you create should also pass the **SUPER test**:

- » **(S) SCARY:** Your goals have to scare you.
- » **(U) UNIFYING:** Your goals need to integrate all aspects of your life, holistically.
- » **(P) PURPOSEFUL:** Your goals need to be connected with your greater calling on earth.
- » **(E) ENERGIZING:** Your goals need to energize you and make you want to jump out of bed and pursue them.
- » **(R) RIDICULOUS:** Your goals should make you laugh a little.

→ Having SUPER goals that excite and captivate us will elevate our level of performance. If we want to perform at the highest level, we need to continually be stretching ourselves to higher and higher standards, and we do this through Go Next-Level SUPER goal-setting.

→ **Be skeptical of your own motivation** and ambition. If your motivation and ambition is not attached to actionable goals, you will be let down and stuck on plateaus. Only with Go Next-Level Goals, will you launch to unimaginable accomplishments.

→ Many people in life have big dreams, but it's only those who can take those big dreams and convert them into bite-sized actional steps that will result in success.

→ Staying committed to goals are the fruits and veggies version of your aspirational life. **Disciplined commitment** provides the essential nutrients, but isn't as much fun to eat. But without these nutrients of clear goals, pursued with discipline, we will never Go-Next-Level and launch from the plateau.

CHAPTER NINE

HOW ARE YOU GOING TO GET THERE?

GO-NEXT-LEVEL BLUEPRINT STEP #9:
DEVELOPING THE GO NEXT-LEVEL HABITS

> Dreams are not easy. Dreams are painful. They force work and commitment.
>
> ROBERT KIYOSAKI

THE *Go Next-Level* BLUEPRINT

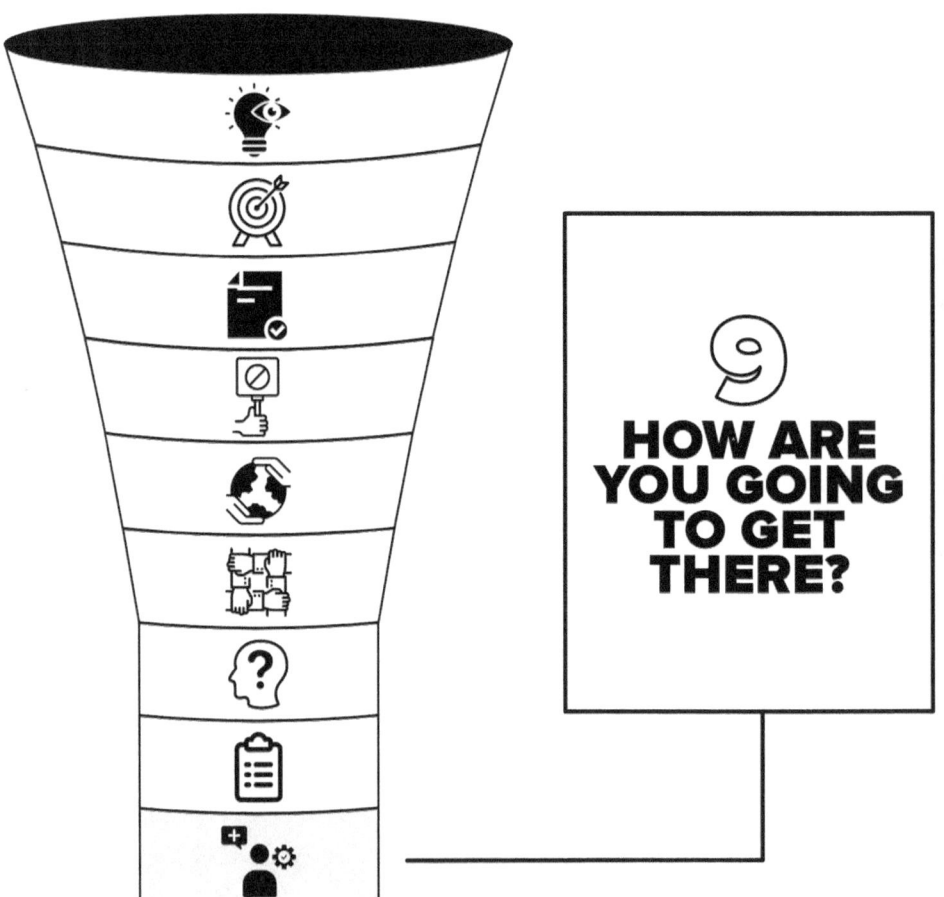

SUCCESS IS NOTHING MORE THAN A CULMINATION OF RIGHT CHOICES

The truth about most people is this: most people are lazy and most people drift through life without intentionality. This is really good news because you are anything but average. You are someone who's not content with the status quo and wants to go to new heights. So, if you are simply willing to work slightly harder than the masses and make very intentional decisions, you will go far places in life and launch off any plateaus. The competition isn't strong. I say this without judgment of anyone else, but simply as a reflection of reality. Most people want to "*get by*" and be "*left alone.*" And so, even a subtle willingness to begin orchestrating your life and business decision making with clarity and intentionality, combined with a little elbow grease, will immediately separate you from the pack. I'm certain you would agree. Most people who remain stuck on the plateau and unable to launch to new levels are stuck there for one of two reasons: either they are *not willing* to go the extra mile to get unstuck, or they are *not clear about how* to get unstuck. If you are reading this, one thing I know about you is that you're not lazy. Lazy people don't read books like this. So, imagine then for a second what is possible for you when you layer the prior eight chapters of the Go Next-Level Blueprint **on top of building a proven habit system**; the world will become your oyster. You know how to work hard, now we have to make sure we're doing the right kind of hard work.

We can architect an Ideal Life, create a vision, build a Life-Team, and do all the things that we need to do leading up to this point, but the truth is, unless we're willing to create the smart daily choices day-in and day-out, which become habits, none of our dreams and ambitions will come to fruition. **After all, your level of success is simply a culmination of your daily choices, which done repetitively over time, become habits that either move you closer to or farther away from your Ideal Life.** There are no shortcuts in life and business, but when we implement the right daily choices that ultimately become habits, it becomes a bit of a cheat code.

In this final chapter of the Go Next-Level Blueprint, we'll get more sophisticated and nuanced about what it means to *"work hard"* in regards to habit formation, which is a necessary ingredient in launching you off the plateau. More than simply *"working hard"*, which can often yield low results, we're going to talk about a very specific version of working hard by developing Go Next-Level Habits.

HARD WORK + INTENTIONALITY CREATES GO NEXT-LEVEL RESULTS

My client Jay is a very famous YouTuber that built a multi-million person following on social media as a business coach, and a master of habits that have yielded him great results. Up at 4 a.m., every single moment of the day was meticulously accounted for. From the morning routine and ice-baths, to the time-blocking to create new content, to the deliberate meetings with his staff, to the business development strategy sessions, to end-of-day meditation rituals, there wasn't a wasted moment. Jay's success was the living proof that hard-work combined with focused intentionality paid big dividends.

 Jay was a great example of what was possible with the right kind of habits.

What I learned from Jay wasn't that people needed to *"work hard"* to achieve great things. What Jay taught me was the need for massive amounts of intentionality, combined with the hard work, which ultimately become habits. He showed me that hard work without intentionality left people busy but unproductive. But hard work, combined with intentionality, left people accomplished with

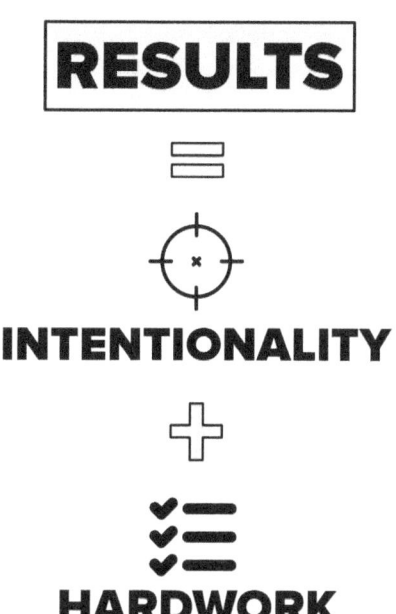

big results. Reaching the Go Next-Level summit requires a willingness to work hard, yes, but also a strategic intentionality with our hard work. Our aim is not busyness, but results. Hard work without focused intentionality creates unproductive busyness and low-level results.

EVERYONE WANTS TO BE SUCCESSFUL BUT FEW ARE WILLING TO PAY THE PRICE

We see bumper stickers and Instagram memes every day saying things like, "*Live Your Best Life*", "*You Got This*", "*You Are Stronger Than You Think*", or some version of a motivational quip that gets people excited about doing something great. I'm not knocking these quotes but they are a bit of a lie. What gets left out of the quote is how much work it takes to actually live your best life. Living your best life requires a tremendous amount of self-sacrifice, inward looking, paradigm stretching, discipline, and delayed gratification.

Most people will actually never live their best life; because they aren't willing to do these hard things. Most people will be challenged with saying *"no"* to the ease and comfort of the good-enough now, in exchange for the *"yes"* of intentional hard work for sake of something greater in the future.

These quotes can give people the impression that attaining your best life might be possible if you're simply motivated enough. If you just believe the quote enough and keep telling yourself that *"you are stronger than you think"*, then maybe you'll become stronger than you think. If it was only that easy. We can accidentally and wrongly give people an idea that success might be easy. And some level of success is, in fact, fairly easy. But if you want to go to unprecedented levels in your life or business, driven by your Ideal Life in Chapter One, it's going to require a certain kind of hard work in habit formation only a few are willing to pay the price for.

My client, Issac, is a real estate agent on his own Go Next-Level journey. Feeling plateaued by the slowdown in the market, he knows he needs to make some changes to elevate his business. Up to this point, Issac has been very successful but, due to changing market conditions, what has worked for him up to this point in creating success, no longer works. On his own Go Next-Level journey, he's being forced to look at himself, his business, and make some important changes.

Recently, Isaac was telling me how much he struggles with video marketing and that he's never had to do any of it up to this point of his career. But he understands the power in it and realizes that if he wants to take his business to the next level, he needs to pursue this marketing angle. But he's shy, hates being on camera, and feels self-conscious and anxious. He avoided video marketing like the plague, and kept looking for other marketing avenues that were *"more comfortable"*.

I explained to Isaac that he simply had two choices: he could press into his fears, overcome his anxiety about being on camera and become a next-level real estate person, or he could settle for a mediocre business and feel stuck on the plateau. And the more time he spent looking for a magic third alternative to a marketing solution was precious time wasted he could be moving in the right direction. He needed to make a decision.

> **CRITICAL INSIGHT:** At some point for all of us, our vision of Go Next-Level will collide with what we don't want to do; This fork in the road will determine if you stay stuck on a plateau or if you launch to Go Next-Level.

Going to the next level and fulfilling high levels of success requires a willingness to embrace discomfort. There are no shortcuts, hacks, or three-step formulas to get around this fact. The more we shy away from hard things, the more we stay stuck on the plateau.

> **What intentional hard work are you avoiding, that is keeping you stuck on any plateaus?**

I'VE BROUGHT YOU TO WATER. ARE YOU READY TO DRINK?

This is the final stop in the Go Next-Level Blueprint, and this section will separate those who are truly ready to launch from any plateaus and those who are not. This chapter is where the rubber meets the road; you either remain stuck on the plateau, or launch to new heights and crazy levels of success, depending on your willingness to do the necessary hard things.

A secret I've learned from my coaching business is that when I'm considering taking on a new client, I will give them a very simple and easy homework assignment before I commit to them or they commit to me. The assignments I give them are always relevant to their growth, so it's never a waste of time, and it's always easy. The people who complete the assignment always become great clients, and the ones that don't do the assignment I usually pass on working with. Over the years I've learned that clients unwilling to do the heavy lifting always become bad clients. The people ready and willing to do the heavy lifting are the people I can help the most. Otherwise, it's always some version of "forcing a horse to drink".

> *"In every situation, life is asking us a question, and our actions are the answer."*
>
> **RYAN HOLIDAY**

 What questions are you answering with your actions?

THE HABITS OF GO NEXT-LEVEL PEOPLE

What is a habit? A habit is nothing more than an unconscious decision. Everybody has habits; some are good habits that promote great lives and some are bad habits that promote setbacks. Habits are formed by repetitive daily decisions, over time, that eventually become subconscious and automatic. We all have habits, and to Go Next-Level, we have to develop the right kinds of habits that will get us unstuck from any plateaus and launch us to new levels. **When we combine the right kind of hard work with focused intentionality, overtime, it becomes a Go Next-Level Habit.**

To go to the next level in life and business, we have to develop certain habits that have been proven to optimize the highest functioning and highest yielding results for life and business. When we look at Go Next-Level people across a wide spectrum of domains from business, to parenting, to marriage, to health, to wealth, we see tried and true habits being employed that have been proven to yield the best results. These habits are what separate them from other people who remain stuck on plateaus. To Go Next-Level, there are **ten habits** that we must begin building. These habits, which begin as simple daily choices, done repetitively over time, become subconscious ways of living that yield the highest results. *This is the right kind of hard work + focused intentionality.*

THE 10 ESSENTIAL GO NEXT-LEVEL HABITS

HABIT #1: Do what's hard first.
To Go Next-Level, develop the habit of planning your day around doing the hard things first. While most people do what feels good first, people who are skyrocketing off plateaus do the opposite. Human beings love easy and comfortable, and Go Next-Level people fight the temptation for easy and comfortable and develop the habit of pursuing what's most challenging. Not because they are masochists, but because they know this is where the most fruit is produced. Your to-do list each day should start with the hardest thing you need to do that day.

HABIT #2: Prioritize physical health.
Prioritizing your physical health is the base of the pyramid for optimal success. And if you want to accomplish what you need to accomplish to Go Next-Level, you need your focus, mental clarity, stamina, and energy levels as high as possible, and the only way to do that is to prioritize your physical health. Go Next-Level people place an inordinate amount of time and dedication toward diet, sleep, exercise, and physical wellness. Brain power is a derivative of physical health, and with 73% of America being overweight, it's no wonder so few people are accomplishing what they are capable of.

HABIT #3: Create structure & routine.

Humans are creatures of habit. And the more structure and routine we can create, the easier it becomes to develop the Go Next-Level Habits. Structure and routine keep us focused and on task. Instead of developing decision fatigue and re-inventing the wheel day after day, you operate best inside a container of structure and routine. According to research, 92% of highly successful people have a morning routine. When others don't want to be confined by a structure, Go Next-Level people separate themselves from the pack by intentionally creating structure. Create structure and routine by time blocking everything on your calendar from work, to fun, to family. Structure and plan for "unstructured" time as well.

HABIT #4: Keep your house in order.

If you are trying to build your Ideal Life, it's essential your personal world is harmoniously balanced with your professional world. Go Next-Level people develop habits around prioritizing their most important relationships. Strained relationships are the single biggest distraction and energy drain that keeps people stuck on the plateau. Instead of letting out-of-sync relationships rob you of precious mental bandwidth, Go Next-Level people make it a habit to keep their most important relationships on track.

HABIT #5: Prioritize personal development.

Most people stop learning when they graduate college, but not people who Go Next-Level. They are always growing and learning and expanding. It is estimated that 88% of the ultra-wealthy people devote at least thirty minutes to reading per day. While most people are mindlessly scrolling Instagram, Go Next-Level people are learning something new that adds value to their lives and the lives of others.

HABIT #6: Tune-out distractions.

Go Next-Level people don't let the world bombard them with stimulus vying for their attention. They avoid these distractions like the plague and stay focused on their goals. Distractions provide dopamine rewards to the brain, so we naturally want more of it. To Go Next-Level, we have to *embrace the habit of delayed gratification* of these distractions for something more important that we're working toward in the future. That rectangle thing in your pocket right now is a giant detriment to your productivity if you don't ruthlessly manage it.

HABIT #7: Prioritize emotional well-being.
People who have risen to the top in life and business are masters at making sure their emotional equilibrium is balanced. Working toward achieving great things can be massively stressful and exhausting unless you prioritize well-being. Many people make it half-way up the ladder of life, only to burnout and crash, because they did not prioritize their emotional health. To Go Next-Level, make a habit of carving out time for intentionally recharging your batteries through self-care principles. The most successful people are not only the hardest working, but also the hardest working on managing their stress.

HABIT #8: Be a Generous Go-Giver.
People who Go Next-Level have a habit of being generous go-givers. They are always in service to someone or something else other than themselves. If you want to architect your Ideal Life and fulfill everything you want, you have to make sure that you're being a generous go-giver along the way. Most people are go-getters, and have a transactional world-view bent to how they can get more from others. People who skyrocket from plateaus focus on giving more to others than they receive.

HABIT #9: Make people the priority.
Nearly everything starts and ends with relationships. Life at its core is all about relationships. And so it's no surprise to think that we need to prioritize relationships to launch to new levels in life and

business. In life and business, it's never the smartest person in the room who makes the most money or who has the most success, it's the person who's most connected. When people reach pinnacles of success, the sure thing they will tell you is that it was built on the backs of key relationships. Go Next-Level by making it a habit to prioritize your network.

HABIT #10: Be an optimistic problem solver.
Every day, you will be presented with challenges, and you need to develop the habit of responding to those challenges as an optimistic problem solver. Become a person that finds solutions with a nudge of hope and encouragement. If you notice, everyone around you is shrouded with negativity, and you separate yourself from everyone else by being the kind of person that sees the world differently. In a pessimistic world, to Go Next-Level, you have to develop the habit of being an optimistic problem solver.

These ten habits will begin to separate you from others and help you move to your own next level. The ten Go Next-Level Habits might seem easy, but it's important to remember that 99% of the world won't do them. ***These ten Go Next-Level Habits are proven to be the most effective in producing the highest levels of success in business and life.*** They are the most obvious and practical ways to distinguish yourself from other people who will remain stuck on the plateau.

Remember, good habit formation can be boiled down to delayed gratification and impulse control. Can we *do* the habits that are good, even when it doesn't *feel* good? The more you're able to override the monkey brain that seeks pleasure in the moment for something better in the future, the more you're going to begin launching from any plateaus. Start incorporating these ten habits today, and you'll be exponentially faster in moving toward getting unstuck and launching to new levels.

> *"Success is nothing more than a few simple disciplines, practiced every day."*
>
> **JIM ROHN**

GO NEXT-LEVEL HABIT FORMATION

The ten Go Next-Level Habits are where the rubber meets the road on the Go Next-Level journey. All the dreaming and planning and ambition are essential, but there will come a time when you have to simply make ***one small decision*** on how you are going to spend your time. This is the biggest fork in the road that separates those who build their Ideal Life, and those who don't. Let's look at a few questions so you can assess how you might need to evolve in this area.

- How would you rate your impulse control? Are you willing to say "no" to the easy things in the moment and delay gratification for something better in the future?
- When it comes to simply getting things done, would the people close to you say you're willing to go the extra mile? Or do you look for shortcuts to avoid the suffering that is required to get to the top anywhere in your life?
- If you're being honest with yourself, is your physical health aligned with your most ambitious goals elsewhere?
- When you look at your calendar, do you see a systematic routine, day-in and day-out, with tons of structure to help with your productivity? Or do your days feel fluid, unstructured, and spontaneous? Remember, massive success requires massive structure because humans operate best in containers of routine.
- There's nothing that will impede your success faster than dysfunctional relationships. How are your most intimate

relationships functioning, and are these relationships catapulting you toward success, or inhibiting your success due to toxic stress and distraction?
- » Do you have a clear and concise morning and evening routine? It's less important what exactly you do for your routines, but that you have one and you're clear about what works best for you.
- » How would you rate your overall stress levels and your ability to emotionally find your equilibrium? Do the people close to you think you take good care of yourself emotionally?
- » Dissociative activities such as over-eating, consuming alcohol, binge-watching television, mindlessly scrolling social media, and pornography are all signs of toxic stress in your body. Do you struggle with any of these?

Developing the ten Go Next-Level Habits that will get you unstuck from the plateau and running toward your Ideal Life is hard work. If you've gotten this far reading the book, you know how to work hard in the traditional sense, but it's a new kind of hard work with the development of the ten Go Next-Level Habits that is going to catapult you to the next level.

 Disciplined habits are the bridge between desires and outcomes.

THE WAR BETWEEN THOUGHTS AND FEELINGS

Getting unstuck and reaching the next level requires a change in the habits in our lives that keep us from the success we're looking for. The ten Go Next-Level Habit formation can be difficult because we might have a lifetime of bad habits that are keeping us from the success we desire. Research on habit formation suggests it takes about sixty days to change a habit. All you have to do is give yourself sixty days of creating new neural pathways in your brain that will eventually become new habits.

The reason habits are hard to break is because there is war inside of you between emotion and logic. Your being up to this point has been mostly driven by your emotions, and it has dictated the choices you make throughout your life. If you stop to think about this, you'll see it everywhere. New habit formation requires that we override our emotional worlds with our rational and logical worlds that are congruent with our values that align with the Ideal Life we're trying to create. This takes time, effort, consistency and practice.

For example, if you have worked a long day and come to the end of the day, you are tired, drained, and ready to check out. Your brain is looking for ease and comfort, from an emotional standpoint. You could pour yourself a drink and check out by watching Netflix, but this would be a dissociative activity to satiate your emotions. If you do this routine most nights over a course of sixty days, eventually it will become a bad habit. To break this habit, you have to allow your cognitive ability to override your emotional desires. Instead of drinking and watching Netflix, you spend the evening doing your new routine. It's not going to feel as good as the old habit, but it's a much better choice. *There's a war going on in your mind about what feels right, and what is right.*

 To win the game of Go Next-Level Habit formation, you have to become a critical analyzer of your emotion. When you do, you'll realize your emotional response is not always in service to optimizing your life.

Here are some examples we can all relate to:

Your emotion says, "*eat the donut.*" Your rational brain says, "*but I want to lose 10 lbs.*"

Your emotion says, "*stop here.*" Your rational brain says, "*it's important to finish this.*"

Your emotion says, *"they hurt me."* Your rational brain says, *"take the high road."*

Your emotion says, *"meet them for happy hour."* Your rational brain says, *"but I need good sleep."*

In order for us to develop the ten Go Next-Level Habits, we have to **override our emotions** with better thinking. We have to see our emotions as the primitive parts of our brain looking to expend the minimum amount of calories both physically and mentally. Our emotions are always trying to get us to do less by doing what's easy and/or comfortable. We have to see this for what it is from an evolutionary standpoint, and use our cognitive abilities to help us make better choices that ultimately serve us in the end toward creating the life and business we desire.

STRUCTURE FOR CREATING GO NEXT-LEVEL HABITS

Developing the ten Go Next-Level Habits is totally possible, and it makes it all the easier when you have a framework for success. Below are six ways to make Go Next-Level habit formation a reality in your life. When you incorporate all six of these principles, you'll be on your way to developing the ten Go Next-Level Habits in no time.

1. Eliminate Triggers

When you're working on building the ten habits necessary for the Go Next-Level journey, the first thing you have to do is eliminate any bad-habit triggers that set you up for failure. For example, if you're trying to cut out your drinking in the evening because you want to use that time to plan for the next day during an evening routine, you might need to remove alcohol from your home. Having alcohol less easily accessible will give you a great advantage in changing the habit. Think about the habit you want to change and find the trigger to eliminate it.

2. Plan Ahead

Great habit formation requires that we plan ahead to make habit formation a success. Planning ahead gives us the control over our environment required for success. For example, if you want to develop the Go Next-Level Habit of connecting with people, you have to control your calendar and schedule in such a way that sets you up for success. The more you plan ahead, the more control you have of your environment and surroundings, the more you can give yourself the opportunity to start building good habits. Great habit formation is never spontaneous. It's always planned.

3. Get to the Root

When we've developed bad habits that are working against our success journey, it's important to get to the root of what the bad habit is serving emotionally. For example, if you want to develop the Go Next-Level Habit of daily personal development, but are distracted by responding to endless emails instead, get to the root of what compulsively responding to emails does for you. You might feel overwhelmed and anxious and emails help you feel like you're not falling behind. List all of your bad habits you want to replace and ask yourself what deeper thing the bad habit is serving.

4. Find a Replacement

Developing Go Next-Level habits always requires a replacement. We can't just rip the band-aid off a habit that we've used for a long time without replacing it with another better Go Next-Level Habit. For example, if you have a bad habit of overeating when you are stressed and it's affecting your optimal physical health, you'll need to find replacements such as going on a walk every time you feel the urge to eat. You can't change a bad habit unless you replace it with a good habit.

5. Accountability

To succeed in powerful habit formation, we need accountability partners. We need people in our lives who know the habits we're aiming to develop, and have them check in on us to assess our progress. Developing the ten Go Next-Level Habits isn't easy, and if we're trying to do it alone, it's much more challenging than if we have a team of people supporting us along the way. (Refer back to Life-Team in Chapter Six on the people we need in our lives to make it to the top.)

6. Intrinsic Motivation

And lastly, developing the ten Go Next-Level Habits requires us to be continuously reminded of the *"what"* and the *"why"* for habit development. This points us back to Chapter One and Chapter Two of the Go Next-Level journey where we are reminded of what we want, and why we want it. We need to review these two pieces of information ***every single day*** to keep our minds glued to the intrinsic motivation that is driving new habit formation. Developing great habits is not easy, so we need to be constantly reminded of our driving force to keep us on the journey toward greater things.

Go Next-Level Habit formation requires work. It requires discipline to do the things you likely don't really want to do but need to do in order to reach new levels of success. Bad habit formation is easy and natural, while good habit formation requires intentionality and effort. **To Go Next-Level, understand this Truth: All of life is just a series of small choices you make every day. Those choices become habits, and the habits you have dictate the outcome of your life.**

DISCIPLINE EQUALS FREEDOM

After coaching high-performing people for nearly twenty years, I have learned that this is the decision point for most people in their lives; who's willing to pay the price of delayed gratification, and who's not. People willing to develop positive habits and win the war in their mind choose their values over their emotions. And these are the people who will Go Next-Level.

Discipline, which is another way to talk about delayed gratification, equals *freedom* in life and business. When we don't have control over our habits, our habits end up controlling us. They cause us to work against ourselves and we ultimately become enslaved by emotions telling us to act now on this thing that is not in alignment with our bigger ideal, mission, and purpose. Being willing to challenge the emotional impulses with the better and more powerful ten Go Next-Level Habits is what ultimately gets us to the next level.

 This kind of hard work is done by everyone we have ever admired.

When you are willing to do this hard work in building the ten Go Next-Level Habits, it results in more freedom than we could imagine. Freedom to spend your time exactly the way you want... Freedom to make as much money as you want... Freedom to have the kind of relationships you want... Discipline now results in freedom later.

This is what it means to outwork everyone else. While nearly all of the world is enslaved by their emotional impulses to feel good in the moment, the elite have mastered the discipline required to say "*no*" to something good in the present moment in service to something greater in the future. When we take the prior chapters in the Go Next-Level Blueprint and layer them on top of the ten Go Next-Level Habits, no one can stop your achievement.

A NEW KIND OF HARD WORK

Even with the best planning, dreaming, and relentless ambition, we have to be willing to put in the work. But it's more than a simple idea of "work hard" where we might associate the idea with longer hours, grinding, and late nights burning the candle at both ends to finish a project. Sure, there might be some of that from time to time, but the "hard work" required to reach the Go Next-Level summit is specifically about developing the discipline for the ten Go Next-Level Habits.

When we look at most of the world and see the billions of people who will never tap into their true potential, we'll always see an unwillingness of those people to say "no" to the delayed gratification for something better in the future. To Go Next-Level, we have to be willing to say "*no*" to the *good* thing now, for the sake of being able to say "*yes*" to the *great* thing in the future. It is this discipline of delayed gratification that will catapult you toward the highest levels of any definition of success you're desiring.

To Go Next-Level, we need to continually analyze our lives looking for bad habits that are keeping us stuck which need to be replaced with the right habits.

Every day we simply walk through life making one choice after the other. And it's this simple act of which choices you will make that will influence the course of your life and your success. These choices, overtime, become the habits driving your life. We all have habits, and it's the work of anyone desiring to get unstuck from any and all plateaus to make sure all our daily choices, which become habits, are in service to the picture we painted in our Ideal Life.

 If I conducted an audit of your daily choices, would it support what you said you wanted in Chapter One?

GO NEXT-LEVEL ACTION STEP:

Get out your pen and journal and review the ten Go Next-Level Habits earlier in this chapter. Journal through the ten habits and ask yourself where you are excelling in those habits, and where you need an overhaul in those habits.

GO NEXT-LEVEL KEY-TAKEAWAYS

CHAPTER NINE: "How Are You Going To Get There?"

- Most people who remain stuck on the plateau and unable to launch to new levels are stuck there for one of **two reasons**:
  » either they are not willing to go the extra mile to get unstuck,
  » or they are not clear about how to get unstuck.

- We can architect an Ideal Life, create a vision, build a Life-Team, and do all the things that we need to do leading up to this point, but the truth is, unless we're willing to create the **smart daily choices day-in and day-out**, which become habits, none of our dreams and ambitions will come to fruition.

- Your level of success is simply a **culmination of your daily choices**, which done repetitively over time, become habits that either move you closer to or farther away from your Ideal Life.

- Hard work without focused intentionality creates **unproductive busyness** and low-level results.

- **Most people will be challenged** with saying "no" to the ease and comfort of the good-enough now, in exchange for the "yes" of intentional hard work for sake of something greater in the future.

- At some point for all of us, our vision of Go Next-Level will collide with what we don't want to do; **this fork in the road** will determine if you stay stuck on a plateau or if you launch to Go Next-Level.

→ Going to the next level and fulfilling high levels of success requires a willingness to **embrace discomfort.** There are no shortcuts, hacks, or three-step formulas to get around this fact. The more we shy away from hard things, the more we stay stuck on the plateau.

→ To go to the next level in life and business, we have to develop certain habits that have been proven to optimize the highest functioning and **highest yielding results** for life and business.

→ When we look at Go Next-Level people across a wide spectrum of domains from business, to parenting, to marriage, to health, to wealth, **we see tried and true habits** being employed that have been proven to yield the best results. These habits are what separate them from other people who remain stuck on plateaus.

→ These habits, which begin as simple daily choices, done repetitively over time, become subconscious ways of living that yield the highest results. This is the right kind of hard work + focused intentionality.

- » **HABIT #1:** Do what's hard first.
- » **HABIT #2:** Prioritize physical health.
- » **HABIT #3:** Create structure & routine.
- » **HABIT #4:** Keep your house in order.
- » **HABIT #5:** Prioritize personal development.
- » **HABIT #6:** Tune-out distractions.
- » **HABIT #7:** Prioritize emotional well-being.
- » **HABIT #8:** Be a Generous Go-Giver.
- » **HABIT #9:** Make people the priority.
- » **HABIT #10:** Be an optimistic problem solver.

→ These habits are the **most practical ways** to distinguish yourself from other people who will remain stuck on the plateau.

→ Good habit formation can be boiled down to **delayed gratification** and **impulse control**. Can we do the habits that are good, even when it doesn't feel good? The more you're able to override the monkey brain that seeks pleasure in the moment for something better in the future, the more you're going to begin launching from any plateaus.

→ Disciplined habits are the **bridge** between desires and outcomes.

→ To win the game of Go Next-Level Habit formation, you have to become a critical analyzer of your emotion. When you do, you'll realize your emotional response is not always in service to optimizing your life.

→ To Go Next-Level, understand this Truth: All of life is just a **series of small choices** we make every day. Those choices become habits, and **the habits you have dictate the outcome of your life**.

→ Discipline, which is another way to talk about delayed gratification, equals freedom in life and business. When we don't have control over our habits, our habits end up controlling us. They cause us to work against ourselves and we ultimately **become enslaved by emotions** telling us to act now on this thing that is not in alignment with our bigger ideal, mission, and purpose.

→ To Go Next-Level, we need to continually analyze our lives looking for bad habits that are keeping us stuck which need to be replaced with the right habits.

> The future has several names. For the weak, it is impossible; For the fainthearted, it is unknown: But for the valiant, it is ideal.
>
> VICTOR HUGO

CONCLUSION

START GOING NEXT-LEVEL, TODAY

One cool fall morning, my wife and I sat on the front porch of our house talking about life and all the crazy things happening when you're trying to homeschool your kids and run several businesses. As the leaves fell around and the wind sang its gusty tune, our conversation divulged into many glorious tangents. We smiled brightly as we spoke of politics, world views, and many other topics typical for our early morning conversations.

Feeling reflective, I looked to my wife and said, *"You know what I'm really grateful for, Hillery?"*

"Me, of course," she said without missing a beat.

"Of course," I said, "but I'm talking beyond us."

"Well, I could take a guess, but I'll let you tell me. You're smiling about something, so what is it?"

"All of those who have helped me get to where I am right now. It's truly an incredible gift. In fact, I'm feeling a growing need, an internal obligation if you will, to pay it forward. I really want to help other people with what I know works to get what we have."

I finished with a sweeping gesture of my arms, hugging her up in the process.

"You've come a long way," Hillery replied as she kissed me. "I've seen what you've had to overcome to get this far."

"I think I need to share with the world the recipe for success that's been given to me by so many great people."

"You should do that, the world would be lucky to have that," she said.

On that very day I started writing the draft of this book. Since then I've labored long and hard over the work in your hands. But it's all for naught if you don't take action. I can't express strongly enough that if you don't push these Nine Questions to the forefront of your life, you'll reach death having missed your one chance to make an impact. It sounds harsh, but it's true.

It doesn't matter where you come from, your background, or any other part of your history. It only matters what you are willing to do from this moment forward. If you follow this Blueprint and apply it to any part of your life and work through the Nine Questions, you will get unstuck from any plateau you find yourself on, and gain a new level of success, whatever that definition is for you. You will surprise everyone around you, including yourself.

I know this formula works. I've coached thousands of people through this exact process. Once finished, they always emerge victorious with massive transformation.

I've also seen many people struggle to take off. They languish in their sameness, too distracted, exhausted, and skeptical to bet on themselves. They don't do the work, so they stay stuck. This could be you. But I know you don't want this for your life. You want to reach the highest heights possible for yourself.

I recognize the swirling thoughts and overwhelm that comes from finishing a book. All of this sounds great, but moving from theory to real life is something else entirely. My suggestion? Take it slow. Answer these questions honestly and then implement them over time. Don't let your fear of starting keep you from making incremental progress.

If you take away nothing else from this book, here are the Nine Questions again along with a quick-start action step for each:

1. **WHAT DO YOU WANT?** You need to create a compelling vision for your business and your life.
2. **WHY DO YOU WANT IT?** You need to have a clear purpose that powerfully motivates you.

3. **WHAT DO YOU NEED TO SAY "YES" TO?** You have to start taking calculated, and appropriate risks.
4. **WHAT DO YOU NEED TO SAY "NO" TO?** You have to start implementing boundaries to ruthlessly protect your time.
5. **HOW ARE YOU GOING TO SAVE THE WORLD?** You need to identify your unique mission that changes the lives of others.
6. **WHO IS GOING WITH YOU?** You need a special team of people that you intentionally appoint as council of your life.
7. **WHO DO YOU THINK YOU ARE?** You have to cultivate a mindset of unshakable self-belief.
8. **WHAT IS THE PLAN?** You need to become a master SUPER goal-setter and reach for the stars.
9. **HOW ARE YOU GOING TO GET THERE?** You have to cultivate the life-changing, ten Go Next-Level Habits.

Thank you so much for reading all the way to the end of this book. By doing so, you've already set yourself apart from the vast majority of people who buy books in the hopes that it will empower them as it sits on their bookshelf, unread and collecting dust.

You've got what it takes to Go Next-Level. Now, go get it.

QUENTIN

PS: I truly want to hear about your Go Next-Level journey. Please send me a message at info@quentinhafner.com.
PPS: Please visit www.QuentinHafner.com/GoNextLevel for more information and resources on taking your business and life to the next level.

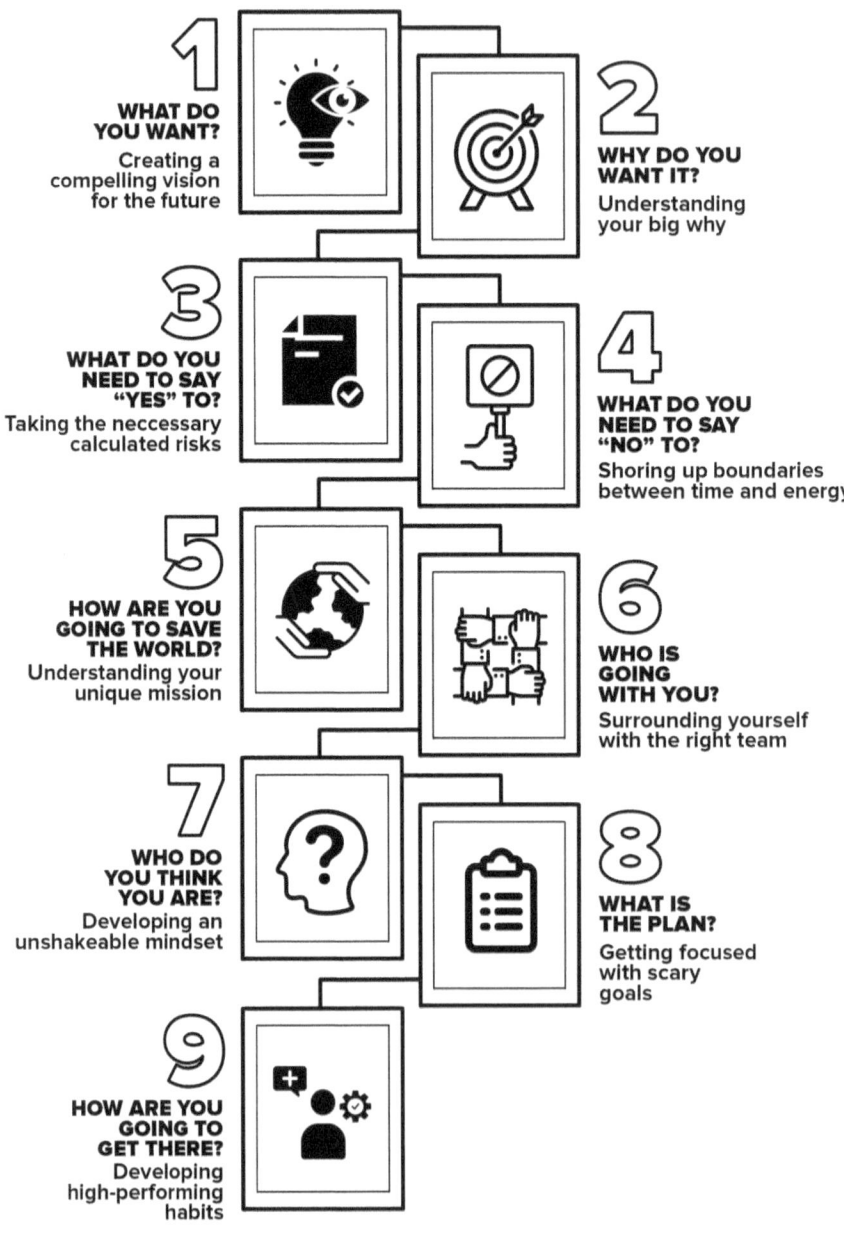

www.ingramcontent.com/pod-product-compliance
Lightning Source LLC
Chambersburg PA
CBHW060558080526
44585CB00013B/613